grzimek's
Student Animal Life Resource

• • • •

grzimek's
Student Animal Life Resource

● ● ● ●

Cumulative Index

Madeline S. Harris, project editor

Neil Schlager and Jayne Weisblatt, editors

THOMSON

GALE

Detroit • New York • San Francisco • San Diego • New Haven, Conn. • Waterville, Maine • London • Munich

THOMSON
—★—
GALE
™

Grzimek's Student Animal Life Resource: Cumulaitive Index

Project Editor
Madeline S. Harris

Editorial
Stephanie Cook, Kathleen J. Edgar, Melissa Hill, Kristine Krapp, Elizabeth Manar, Heather Price, Lemma Shomali, Mark Springer

Indexing Services
Synapse, the Knowledge Link Corporation

Rights and Acquisitions
Margaret Abendroth, Timothy Sisler

Imaging and Multimedia
Randy Bassett, Michael Logusz, Dan Newell, Chris O'Bryan, Robyn Young

Product Design
Tracey Rowens, Jennifer Wahi

Composition
Evi Seoud, Mary Beth Trimper

Manufacturing
Wendy Blurton, Dorothy Maki

LIBRARY OF CONGRESS CATALOGING-IN-PUBLICATION DATA

Grzimek's student animal life resource. Cumulative index / Madeline S. Harris, project editor.
    p. cm.
  ISBN 0-7876-9403-7 (softcover)
  1. Grzimek's student animal life resource—Indexes—Juvenile literature. I. Harris, Madeline S. II. Grzimek's student animal life resource.
  Z7991.G79 2006
  [QL49]
  590—dc22   2005018810

ISBN 0-7876-9402-9 (21-vol set), ISBN 0-7876-9403-7

This title is also available as an e-book
Contact your Thomson Gale sales representative for ordering information.

Printed in United States of America
10 9 8 7 6 5 4 3 2 1

Index

Italic type indicates volume; **boldface** type indicates main entries and their pages; (ill.) indicates illustrations.

A indicates the Amphibians volumes 1-3.
B indicates the Birds volumes 1-5.
CJ indicates Corals, Jellyfishes, Sponges and Other Simple Animals volume.
CM indicates Crustaceans, Mollusks, and Segmented Worms volume.
F indicates the Fishes volume.
I indicates the Insects and Spiders volumes 1-2.
M indicates the Mammals volumes 1-5.
R indicates the Reptiles volumes 1-2.

A

Aardvarks, *M 1:* 9, *M 4:* 804–807, 805 (ill.), 806 (ill.)
Aardwolves, *M 3:* 580, 649–656, 654 (ill.), 655 (ill.)
Abaco boas, *R 2:* 342

Abalones, *CM* 261
Abbott's boobies, *B 1:* 126
Abderitidae, *M 1:* 39
Abrocoma cinerea. See Ashy chinchilla rats
Abrocomidae. See Chinchilla rats
Abyssinian ground-hornbills, *B 3:* 653–654
Acanthaster planci. See Crown-of-thorns
Acanthisitta chloris. See Riflemen
Acanthisittidae. See New Zealand wrens
Acanthixalus spinosus. See African wart frogs
Acanthiza chrysorrhoa. See Yellow-rumped thornbills
Acanthizidae. See Australian warblers
Acanthocephala. See Thorny-headed worms
Acanthophis antarcticus. See Death adders
Acanthuroidei, *F* 326–333
Acanthurus lineatus. See Lined surgeonfishes
Accentors. *See* Hedge sparrows
Accipitridae. *See* Eagles; Hawks

Aceros cassidix. See Sulawesi red-knobbed hornbills
Acherontia atropos. See Death's head hawk moths
Acipenseriformes. *See* Paddlefishes; Sturgeons
Acoela. *See* Acoels
Acoels, *CJ* 74–77
Acomys cahirinus. See Egyptian spiny mice
Acorn barnacles, *CM* 196
Acorn worms, *CJ* 241–242
Acridotheres tristis. See Common mynas
Acrobates pygmaeus. See Pygmy gliders
Acrobatidae. See Feather-tailed possums
Acrochordidae. *See* File snakes
Acrochordus granulatus. See Little file snakes
Actenoides concretus. See Rufous-collared kingfishers
Actinodura sodangorum. See Black-crowned barwings
Action Plan for Australian Birds, *B 4:* 1081
Actophilornis africanus. See African jacanas
Acutotyphlops subocularis, *R 2:* 302

Acyrthosiphon pisum. See Pea aphids

Adaptation and twisted-wing parasites, *I 2:* 317

Adders
    death, *R 2:* 414, 415, 416, 423–424, 423 (ill.), 424 (ill.)
    dwarf puff, *R 2:* 380
    night, *R 2:* 382
    See also Eastern hog-nosed snakes

Adelotus brevis. See Tusked frogs

Adenophores. *See* Roundworms

Aechmophorus occidentalis. See Western grebes

Aedes aegypti. See Yellow fever mosquitoes

Aegithalidae. *See* Long-tailed titmice

Aegithina tiphia. See Common ioras

Aegotheles insignis. See Feline owlet-nightjars

Aegothelidae. *See* Owlet-nightjars

Aepyronis maximus. See Elephant birds

Aequipecten opercularis. See Queen scallops

Aequorea victoria, CJ 50, 50 (ill.)

Aethopyga species, *B 5:* 1209

Afghan pikas, *M 5:* 1206

Africa bay owls, *B 3:* 559

African black oystercatchers, *B 2:* 418, 419

African broadbills, *B 4:* 796–797, 796 (ill.), 797 (ill.)

African bulbuls. *See* Common bulbuls

African bullfrogs, *A 2:* 287, 289–291

African burrowing snakes, *R 2:* 393–398

African chevrotains, *M 4:* 927

African civets, *M 3:* 631–633, 631 (ill.), 632 (ill.)

African clawed frogs. *See* Common plantannas

African elephants, *M 4:* 813, 815, 816, 819

African finfoot, *B 2:* 366–368

African flycatchers, *B 4:* 1060, 1061

African gray parrots. *See* Gray parrots

African heart-nosed bats, *M 2:* 280

African hedgehogs, *M 2:* 218

African hunting wolves, *M 3:* 584

African jacanas, *B 2:* 404–405, 404 (ill.), 405 (ill.)

African linsangs, *M 3:* 629

African mole-rats, *M 5:* 998, 1103–1110

African mud turtles, *R 1:* 70

African mudfishes, *F* 79, 80

African palm swifts, *B 3:* 621–622, 621 (ill.), 622 (ill.)

African paradise-flycatchers, *B 5:* 1117–1119, 1117 (ill.), 1118 (ill.)

African pittas, *B 4:* 812–813, 812 (ill.), 813 (ill.)

African rhinoceroses, *M 4:* 850

African sheath-tailed bats, *M 2:* 305

African side-necked turtles, *R 1:* 70–75, 81

African snipes, *B 2:* 457–458, 457 (ill.), 458 (ill.)

African treefrogs, A 2: 325, **A 3: 331–349**

African wart frogs, **A 3:** 333, 334, 335–336, 346–348, 346 (ill.), 347 (ill.)

African wild cats, *M 3:* 658

African wild dogs, *M 3:* 583

African Wildlife Foundation, *M 4:* 876

Afrixalus brachycnemis, **A 3:** 334

Afro-American river turtles, *R 1:* 81–86

Afrotheria, *M 2:* 216, *M 5:* 1224

Agama hispida. See Spiny agamas

Agamidae, *R 1:* 145–155

Agamodon anguliceps, R 1: 211–212, 211 (ill.), 212 (ill.)

Agelaioides badius. See Baywings

Agelaius phoeniceus. See Red-winged blackbirds

Agkistrodon piscivorus. See Cottonmouths

Aglantha digitale, CJ 48–49, 48 (ill.)

Agouti paca. See Pacas

Agouti taczanowskii. See Mountain pacas

Agoutidae. *See* Pacas

Agoutis, *M 5:* 1153–1159, 1160

Agulhas long-billed larks, *B 4:* 905

Ai. See Brown throated three-toed sloths

Ailao moustache toads, **A 1:** 86–88, 86 (ill.), 87 (ill.)

Ailao spiny toads. *See* Ailao moustache toads

Ailuropoda melanoleuca. See Giant pandas

Ailurus fulgens. See Red pandas

Aitu swiftlets, *B 3:* 617

Aix sponsa. See Wood ducks

Aizen, Marcelo, *M 1:* 44

Ajaia ajaja. See Roseate spoonbills

Ajolotes. *See* Mole-limbed wormlizards

Alabama red-bellied turtles, *R 1:* 52

Alabama sturgeons, *F* 34

Alaemon alaudipes. See Greater hoopoe-larks

Alagoas antwrens, *B 4:* 838

Alagoas tyrannulets, *B 4:* 853

Alaotra grebes, *B 1:* 92

Alaudidae. *See* Larks

Albatrosses, *B 1:* 41, 43, 44, 45–52

Albert's lyrebirds, *B 4:* 888–889, 890, 891–893, 891 (ill.), 892 (ill.)

Albula vulpes. See Bonefishes

Albuliformes, *F* 55–59

Alcedinidae. *See* Kingfishers

Alces alces. See Moose

Alcidae. *See* Auks; Murres; Puffins

Alcids, *B 2:* 395, 396

Alderflies, *I 2:* 262–267

Alepisaurus ferox. See Longnose lancetfishes

Alexander, Shana, *M 4:* 811

Alexander the Great and the Gordian knot, *CJ* 144

Alextgeroon jynx, **A** *3:* 337

Allanaspides helonomus. See Tasmanian anaspid crustaceans

Allanaspides hickmani. See Hickman's pygmy mountain shrimps

Alligator gars, *F* 38

Alligator lizards, *R 2:* 260–266

Alligator mississippiensis. See American alligators

Alligator snapping turtles, *R 1:* 34

Alligatoridae. *See* Alligators

Alligators, *R 1:* 101–107, 114–122

Allopauropus carolinensis, I 2: 441, 441 (ill.)

Allophryne ruthveni. See Ruthven's frogs

Allophrynidae. *See* Ruthven's frogs

Allosaurus species, *R 1:* 4

Almiquis. *See* Cuban solenodons

Alouatta seniculus. See Venezuelan red howler monkeys

Alpaca Owners and Breeders Association, *M 4:* 918

Alpacas, *M 4:* **916–926,** 921 (ill.), 922 (ill.)

Alpine marmots, *M 5:* 1017–1018, 1017 (ill.), 1018 (ill.)

Alpine salamanders, **A** *3:* 443

Alpine toads, **A** *1:* 77

Altricial chicks, *B 2:* 321

Alytes obstetricans. See Midwife toads

Amami woodcocks, *B 2:* 456

Amazon poison frogs, **A** *2:* 219, 223

Amazon river dolphins. *See* Botos

Amazon tree boas, *R 2:* 343

Amazonian horned frogs. *See* Surinam horned frogs

Amazonian manatees, *M 4:* 829, 841

Amazonian milk frogs, **A** *2:* 262

Amazonian poison frogs. *See* Amazon poison frogs

Amazonian skittering frogs, **A** *2:* 274–275, 274 (ill.), 275 (ill.)

Amazonian umbrellabirds, *B 4:* 877–878, 877 (ill.), 878 (ill.)

Ambergris, *M 4:* 760

Ambrosia beetles, *I 2:* 296

Ambystoma tigrinum. See Tiger salamanders

Ambystomatidae. *See* Mole salamanders

Ameivas, giant, *R 2:* 236

American alligators, *R 1:* 102, 104–105, 114, 116, 117–119, 117 (ill.), 118 (ill.)

American anhingas, *B 1:* 121–123, 121 (ill.), 122 (ill.)

American avocets, *B 2:* 424, 428–429, 428 (ill.), 429 (ill.)

American beavers. *See* North American beavers

American birch mice, *M 5:* 1047

American bison, *M 4:* 973–975, 973 (ill.), 974 (ill.)

American black bears, *M 3:* 593, 596–598, 596 (ill.), 597 (ill.)

American black rails, *B 2:* 315

American burying beetles, *I 2:* 310–311, 310 (ill.), 311 (ill.)

American Cetacean Society, *M 4:* 707

American chipmunks, *M 5:* 1008

American cliff swallows, *B 4:* 919–921, 919 (ill.), 920 (ill.)

American cockroaches, *I 1:* 111–113, 111 (ill.), 112 (ill.)

American crocodiles, *R 1:* 117, 118, 127–128, 127 (ill.), 128 (ill.)

American dippers, *B 4:* 1005, 1007–1009, 1007 (ill.), 1008 (ill.)

American eels, *F* 62–63, 62 (ill.), 63 (ill.)

American goldfinches, *B 5:* 1282–1284, 1282 (ill.), 1283 (ill.)

American horseshoe crabs, *I 1:* 12–14, 12 (ill.), 13 (ill.)

American leaf-nosed bats, *M 2:* **345–357,** 359

American least shrews, *M 2:* 250–251, 250 (ill.), 251 (ill.)

American mourning doves, *B 3:* 513–514, 513 (ill.), 514 (ill.)

American mud turtles, *R 1:* 10, **64–69**

American musk turtles, *R 1:* 10, **64–69**

American pearl kites, *B 1:* 212

American pikas, *M 5:* 1206, 1208–1209, 1208 (ill.), 1209 (ill.)

American redstarts, *B 4:* 792

American robins, *B 4:* 1014, 1015, 1022–1023, 1022 (ill.), 1023 (ill.)

American saltwater crocodiles. *See* American crocodiles

American shrew-moles, *M 2:* 256

American tailed caecilians, A 3: 506–510

American toads, *A 2:* 199, 200, 201–202

American water shrews, *M 2:* 252–253, 252 (ill.), 253 (ill.)

American white pelicans, *B 1:* 139–141, 139 (ill.), 140 (ill.)

Amero-Australian treefrogs, A 2: 259–286

Amia calva. See Bowfins

Amico, Guillermo, *M 1:* 44

Amiiformes. *See* Bowfins

Ammodytes americanus. See Inshore sand lances

AmphibiaWeb, *A 3:* 355

Amphionidacea. See Amphionids

Amphionides reynaudii, CM 118–120, 120 (ill.)

Amphionids, CM 118–120

Amphipholis squamata. See Dwarf brittle stars

Amphipoda. *See* Amphipods

Amphipods, CM 185–194

Amphisbaena alba. See White-bellied wormlizards

Amphisbaenia, *R 1:* 190, 197, 203, 208

Amphisbaenidae. *See* Wormlizards

Amphiuma tridactylum. See Three-toed amphiumas

Amphiumas, A 3: 494–500

Amphiumidae. *See* Amphiumas

Amplexus, *A 1:* 4, 20
    See also specific species

Amytornis striatus. See Striated grasswrens

Anabantoidei. *See* Labyrinth fishes

Anabas testudineus. See Climbing perches

Anableps anableps. See Largescale foureyes

Anacondas, *R 1:* 140, *R 2:* 342, 343, 350–351, 350 (ill.), 351 (ill.)

Anarrhichthys ocellatus. See Wolf-eels

Anas platyrhynchos. See Mallards

Anaspidacea. *See* Anaspidaceans

Anaspidaceans, CM 104–109

Anaspides tasmaniae, CM 107–108, 107 (ill.), 108 (ill.)

Anatidae. *See* Ducks; Geese; Swans

Anax walsinghami. See Giant darners

Anchialine caves, *CM* 161

Anchoa mitchilli. See Bay anchovies

Anchovies, *F* 73, 74, 76–77, 76 (ill.), 77 (ill.)

Andean condors, *B 1:* 177

Andean flamingos, *B 1:* 201, 202

Andean night monkeys, *M 3:* 511

Andean stilts, *B 2:* 423

Andenomus kandianus, A 2: 203

Andigena hypoglauca. See Gray-breasted mountain-toucans

Aneides lugubris. See Arboreal salamanders

Anemones, CJ 26–41

Angel insects, I 2: 216–221

Angelfishes, freshwater, *F* 279–280, 279 (ill.), 280 (ill.)

Angiostrongylus cantonensis. See Rat lungworms

Angleheads, R 1: 145–155

Anglerfishes, F 187–193

Anglewings, *I 2:* 371

Angling, *F* 188

Anguidae, R 2: 260–266

Anguilla rostrata. See American eels

Anguilliformes. *See* Eels; Morays

Anhima cornuta. See Horned screamers

Anhimidae. *See* Screamers

Anhinga anhinga. See American anhingas

Anhingas, B 1: 98, 99, 116–124

Aniliidae. *See* False coral snakes

Anilius scytale. See False coral snakes

Anilius scytale phelpsorum, R 2: 327

Anilius scytale scytale, R 2: 327

Anis, B 3: 545–551

Annam broad-headed toads, *A 1:* 78, 91–93, 91 (ill.), 92 (ill.)

Annam spadefoot toads. *See* Annam broad-headed toads

Anna's hummingbirds, *B 3:* 636–638, 636 (ill.), 637 (ill.)

Annelida, *CM* 35, 57

Anoles, R 1: 167–176

Anolis carolinensis. See Green anoles

Anomalepididae. *See* Early blind snakes

Anomalepis aspinosus. See South American blind snakes

Anomalepis species, *R 2:* 240

Anomalops katoptron. See Splitfin flashlightfishes

Anomalures, Lord Derby's, *M 5:* 1072–1074, 1072 (ill.), 1073 (ill.)

Anomaluridae. *See* Scaly-tailed squirrels

Anomalurus derbianus. See Lord Derby's anomalures

Anomochilidae. *See* False blind snakes

Anomochilus leonardi, R 2: 309

Anomochilus weberi, R 2: 309

Anoplans, CJ 112–115

Anseriformes, B 2: 241–245

Argentinosaurus species, *R 1*: 2

Argulus foliaceus, CM 210, 212–213, 212 (ill.), 213 (ill.)

Argulus species, *CM* 210

Aristotle and sea squirts, *CJ* 250

Arkansas Department of Environmental Quality, *F* 163

Armadillidium vulgare. See Common pill woodlice

Armadillo lizards, *R 2*: 244

Armadillo officinalis, CM 177

Armadillos, *M 1*: 178–182, **203–211**

Armatobalanus nefrens, CM 198

Armored chameleons, *R 1*: 162–163, 162 (ill.), 163 (ill.)

Armored katydids, *I 1*: 171

Armored rats, *M 5*: 1182

Armyworms, *I 2*: 372

Arnoux's whales, *M 4*: 751

Arothron hispidus. See White-spotted puffers

Arowanas, *F* 47

Arra-jarra-ja. *See* Southern marsupial moles

Arrau. *See* South American river turtles

Arrow worms, CJ 235–240

Arroyo toads, *A 2*: 204

Artamidae. *See* Woodswallows

Artamus cyanopterus. See Dusky woodswallows

Artemia species, *CM* 78

Arthroleptidae. *See* Cricket frogs; Squeakers

Arthroleptinae, *A 2*: 311

Arthroleptis stenodactylus. See Common squeakers

Arthropods, *CM* 57, *I 2*: 269

Articulata, *CM* 317

Artiodactyla. *See* Even-toed ungulates

Ascaphidae. *See* Tailed frogs

Ascaphus montanus. See Rocky Mountain tailed frogs

Ascension frigatebirds, *B 1*: 110

Ascidiacea. *See* Sea squirts

Ascothoracids, *CM* 195–198

Asellia tridens. See Trident leaf-nosed bats

Asexual reproduction, *CJ* 2–3, *CM* 3
   See also specific species

Ash's larks, *B 4*: 905

Ashy chinchilla rats, *M 5*: 1178, 1179–1180, 1179 (ill.), 1180 (ill.)

Asian arowanas. *See* Dragonfishes

Asian bullfrogs. *See* Malaysian painted frogs

Asian chevrotains, *M 4*: 927

Asian dowitchers, *B 2*: 454

Asian elephants, *M 4*: 813–814, 813 (ill.), 814 (ill.), 817

Asian fairy bluebirds, *B 4*: 960–961, 960 (ill.), 961 (ill.)

Asian false vampire bats, *M 2*: 324

Asian frogmouths, *B 3*: 586, 587

Asian giant softshells, *R 1*: 95–96

Asian giant tortoises, *R 1*: 11

Asian grass lizards, *R 2*: 222

Asian horned frogs, *A 1*: 77, 89–90, 89 (ill.), 90 (ill.)

Asian mountain toads, *A 1*: 77, 78, 79

Asian pipe snakes. *See* Pipe snakes

Asian rhinoceroses, *M 4*: 849

Asian river turtles, *R 1*: 11

Asian spadefoot toads. *See* Asian horned frogs

Asian sunbeam snakes. *See* Sunbeam snakes

Asian tailed caecilians, *A 3*: **511–516**

Asian toadfrogs, *A 1*: **77–93**

Asian treefrogs, *A 3*: **350–367**

Asian water dragons, *R 1*: 146

Asiatic black bears, *M 3*: 593, 594, 595

Asiatic giant salamanders, A 3: 419–426

Asiatic rock pythons, *R 2*: 355

Asiatic salamanders, A 3: 409–418

Asiatic water shrews, *M 2*: 213–214

Asities, *B 4*: **801–806,** *B 5*: 1209

Aspidites melanocephalus. See Black-headed pythons

Asplanchna priodonta, CJ 118–119, 118 (ill.), 119 (ill.)

Assa darlingtoni. See Hip pocket frogs

Asses, *M 4*: 848, 850, **854–864**

Asterias amurensis. See Northern Pacific sea stars

Asteroidea. *See* Sea stars

Astley's leiothrix, *B 4*: 1027

Astonishing Elephant (Alexander), *M 4*: 811

Astrapia mayeri. See Ribbon-tailed astrapias

Astrapias, ribbon-tailed, *B 5*: 1391–1392, 1391 (ill.), 1392 (ill.)

Astropecten irregularis. See Sand stars

Astroscopus guttatus. See Northern stargazers

Astylosterninae, *A 2*: 311, 314

Asynchronous hatching, *B 2*: 476

Ateles geoffroyi. See Geoffroy's spider monkeys

Atelidae. *See* Howler monkeys; Spider monkeys

Atelognathus patagonicus. See Patagonia frogs

Atelopus varius. See Harlequin frogs

Atelopus vogli, **A 2**: 203

Atheriniformes. *See*
Rainbowfishes; Silversides
Atherura species, M 5: 1111,
1112
Athroleptinae, A 2: 312
Atlantic bluefin tunas, *F*
338–339, 338 (ill.), 339 (ill.)
Atlantic bottlenosed dolphins.
See Common bottlenosed
dolphins
Atlantic bottlenosed whales.
See Northern bottlenosed
whales
Atlantic cods, F 176–178, 176
(ill.), 177 (ill.)
Atlantic hagfishes, F 3–4, 3
(ill.), 4 (ill.)
Atlantic mantas, F 17–18, 17
(ill.), 18 (ill.)
Atlantic mudskippers, F
322–323, 322 (ill.), 323 (ill.)
Atlantic Ridley seaturtles, R 1:
26
Atlantic salmons, F 131–132,
131 (ill.), 132 (ill.)
Atlantic tarpons, F 52–54, 52
(ill.), 53 (ill.)
Atlas moths, I 2: 385–386, 385
(ill.), 386 (ill.)
Atoll fruit doves, B 3: 505, 509
Atractaspididae. *See* African
burrowing snakes
Atractaspis bibronii. See
Southern burrowing asps
Atrato glass frogs, A 2:
242–243, 247
Atrichornis rufescens. See
Rufous scrub-birds
Atrichornithidae. *See* Scrub-
birds
Attacus atlas. See Atlas moths
Attagis gayi. See Rufous-bellied
seedsnipes
Auckland Island teals, B 2: 241
Audubon, John James, B 4:
852, 933
Auklets, B 2: 486
Auks, B 2: 397, **486–495**

Aulopiformes, F 142–147
Auriparus flaviceps. See Verdins
**Australasian carnivorous
marsupials,** M 1: **51–55,** 75
Australasian figbirds, B 5:
1340–1341, 1340 (ill.), 1341
(ill.)
Australasian larks, B 4:
906–907, 906 (ill.), 907 (ill.)
Australian bell frogs, A 1: 11
Australian Bilby Appreciation
Society, M 1: 77
Australian brush-turkeys, B 2:
270
Australian chats, B 4:
1087–1092
Australian chestnut-backed
buttonquails, B 2: 328
Australian creepers, B 5:
1145–1150
Australian diamond doves, B
3: 504
Australian fairy-wrens, B 4:
1070–1078
Australian false vampire bats,
M 2: 323–328, 326 (ill.), 327
(ill.)
Australian frogmouths, B 3:
585–586, 587
Australian ghost bats. *See*
Australian false vampire bats
Australian greater painted
snipes, B 2: 408, 409, 410,
412
Australian ground frogs, A 1:
124–138, 142
Australian honeyeaters, B 4:
1087, B 5: 1124, **1225–1234**
Australian jumping mice, M 5:
1062–1063, 1062 (ill.), 1063
(ill.)
Australian Koala Foundation,
M 1: 109
Australian magpie-larks, B 5:
1360, 1361, 1362–1364,
1362 (ill.), 1363 (ill.)
Australian magpies, B 5:
1372–1374

Australian masked owls, B 3:
557
Australian owlet-nightjars, B 3:
592, 593
Australian pelicans, B 1: 98,
134
Australian Platypus
Conservancy, M 1: 22
Australian pratincoles, B 2:
436, 437, 442–443, 442 (ill.),
443 (ill.)
Australian pygmy monitors, R
2: 279
Australian robins, B 5:
1123–1129
Australian sea lions, M 3: 674
Australian smelts, F 125–126,
125 (ill.), 126 (ill.)
Australian toadlets, A 1:
139–151
Australian warblers, B 4:
1079–1086
Australian water rats, M 5: 998
Australian whipbirds, B 4:
1099, 1101
**Australo-American side-
necked turtles,** R 1: **18–23**
Austrolebias nigripinnis. See
Blackfin pearl killifishes
Avahis, M 3: **458–465**
Avocets, B 2: **423–430**
Axolotls, A 3: 434
Aye-ayes, M 3: 424, **475–479,**
477 (ill.), 478 (ill.)
Ayu, F 123–124, 123 (ill.),
124 (ill.)
Azara's agoutis, M 5: 1155

B

Babblers, B 4: **1025–1035**
See also Pseudo babblers
Babirusas, M 4: 894, 897–898,
897 (ill.), 899 (ill.)
Baboon lemurs, M 3: 459
Baboons, M 3: 424, 425, 426
Babyrousa babyrussa. See
Babirusas

Bachia bresslaui, R 2: 231–233, 231 (ill.), 232 (ill.)

Bachia species, *R 2:* 228

Bachman's warblers, *B 5:* 1260

Backswimmers, *I 2:* 254–255, 254 (ill.), 255 (ill.)

Bactrian camels, *M 4:* 917, 918

Badgers, *M 3:* 579, **614–627,** 629, 637

Bagworn moths, European, *I 2:* 371

Bahama swallows, *B 4:* 915

Bahaman funnel-eared bats, *M 2:* 379

Bahamian hutias, *M 5:* 1189

Baijis, *M 4:* 707, **714–718,** 716 (ill.), 717 (ill.)

Baird's beaked whales, *M 4:* 751

Balaena mysticetus. See Bowhead whales

Balaeniceps rex. See Shoebills

Balaenicipitidae. *See* Shoebills

Balaenidae. *See* Bowhead whales; Right whales

Balaenoptera acutorostrata. See Northern minke whales

Balaenoptera musculus. See Blue whales

Balaenopteridae. *See* Rorquals

Balanus aguila, CM 198

Bald eagles, *B 1:* 209, *B 2:* 295

Bald uakaris, *M 3:* 516, 520–522, 520 (ill.), 521 (ill.)

Balearica regulorum. See Gray crowned cranes

Baleen whales, *M 4:* 704–706, 777, 783–784, 787, 789, 795

Balistoides conspicillum. See Clown triggerfishes

Ball pythons, *R 2:* 354

Balsam beasts, *I 1:* 179–180, 179 (ill.), 180 (ill.)

Baltimore orioles, *B 5:* 1270–1271, 1270 (ill.), 1271 (ill.)

Bamboo lemurs, *M 3:* 451

Bana leaf litter frogs, *A 1:* 79, 82–83, 82 (ill.), 83 (ill.)

Banana boas. *See* Southern bromeliad woodsnakes

Banana frogs. *See* Golden treefrogs

Band-winged grasshoppers, *I 1:* 169

Banded anteaters. *See* Numbats

Banded archerfishes, *F* 267–268, 267 (ill.), 268 (ill.)

Banded cotingas, *B 4:* 874

Banded geckos, western, *R 1:* 181–182, 181 (ill.), 182 (ill.)

Banded rubber frogs, *A 3:* 387–388, 387 (ill.), 388 (ill.)

Banded stilts, *B 2:* 423

Banded wattle-eyes, *B 4:* 1062

Bandicoots, *M 1:* 74–78, **79–87**
    See also Spiny bandicoots

Banding birds, *B 4:* 852

Bannerman's turacos, *B 3:* 539

Bar-breasted mousebirds, *B 3:* 639, 641–643, 641 (ill.), 642 (ill.)

Barbados raccoons, *M 3:* 581

Barbados yellow warblers, *B 5:* 1260

Barbara's titis, *M 3:* 517

Barbastella barbastellus. See Western barbastelles

Barbastelles, western, *M 2:* 415–416, 415 (ill.), 416 (ill.)

Barbets, *B 3:* 708–709, 725–729, **747–756,** 766, 768

Barbourula busuangensis. See Philippine barbourulas

Barbourulas, *A 1:* **25–43**

Barentsia discreta. See Marine colonial entropocts

Bark beetles, *I 2:* 294, 295, 296

Bark-gnawing beetles, *I 2:* 294

Barklice, *I 2:* **222–226**

Barn owls, *B 3:* 557–563, 564, 565

Barn swallows, *B 4:* 913, 916–918, 916 (ill.), 917 (ill.)

Barnacles, *CM* **195–203**

Barracudas, *F* **334–342**

Barred antshrikes, *B 4:* 836, 840–841, 840 (ill.), 841 (ill.)

Barred bandicoots. *See* Eastern barred bandicoots

Barred buttonquails, *B 2:* 317

Barred eagle-owls, *B 3:* 570–571, 570 (ill.), 571 (ill.)

Barrow, Mary Reid, *B 2:* 247

Basket stars, *CJ* **205–211**

Basses, *F* **256–258,** 261–262, 261 (ill.), 262 (ill.)

Bat bugs, *I 2:* 239

Bat Cave system, *CM* 167–168

Bat flies, *I 2:* 336, 340, 348–349, 348 (ill.), 349 (ill.)

Bates' sunbirds, *B 5:* 1209

Bathyergidae. *See* African mole-rats

Bathynellacea. *See* Bathynellaceans

Bathynellaceans, *CM* **100–103,** 105

Bathynomus giganteus, CM 174

Bathypterois quadrifilis. See Tripodfishes

Batis capensis. See Cape batises

Batrachoidiformes. *See* Toadfishes

Batrachostomus. See Asian frogmouths

Bats, *M 2:* **275–281**
    African giant, *I 1:* 159
    American leaf-nosed, *M 2:* **345–357**
    bulldog, *M 2:* **364–370**
    disk-winged, *M 2:* 384, **388–394,** 396
    false vampire, *M 2:* **323–329**
    free-tailed, *M 2:* 278, 279, **399–408**
    fruit, *M 2:* 277, 280, 282–297, 315, 345
    funnel-eared, *M 2:* **378–382,** 380 (ill.), 381 (ill.), 384
    ghost, *M 2:* **304–311**

Big-eared forest treefrogs, *A 3:* 333, 335–336

Big-headed turtles, *R 1:* 72, **76–80,** 78 (ill.), 79 (ill.), 82–83

Bighorn sheep, *M 4:* 888, 985–987, 985 (ill.), 986 (ill.)

Bilbies, *M 1:* 74–78, **79–87**

Bills and beaks, *B 1:* 146
    See also specific species

Biobot cockroaches, *I 1:* 103

Bioluminescence, *CJ* 27, *I 2:* 295, 427
    See also specific species

Bipedidae. *See* Mole-limbed wormlizards

Bipes biporus. See Two-legged wormlizards

Birch mice, *M 5:* **1044–1050**

Bird fleas, *I 2:* 328

BirdLife International, *B 1:* 62

Birds' nest sponges, *CJ* 6–7, 6 (ill.), 7 (ill.)

Birds of paradise, *B 4:* 789, *B 5:* **1389–1397**

Birds of prey, diurnal, *B 1:* **207–211,** *B 3:* 555, *B 5:* 1346

Birdwing butterflies, *I 2:* 366, 372

Bishops, *B 5:* 1306
    red, *B 5:* 1309
        southern red, *B 5:* 1315–1316, 1315 (ill.), 1316 (ill.)
        yellow-crowned, *B 5:* 1309

Bishop's oos, *B 5:* 1229–1230, 1229 (ill.), 1230 (ill.)

Bison, *M 4:* **969–987**

Bison bison. See American bison

Bites, snake, *R 2:* 382

Bitterns, *B 1:* 143, 146, **149–159**

Bivalves, *CM* **274–288**

Bivalvia. *See* Bivalves

Black-and-red broadbills, *B 4:* 798–800, 798 (ill.), 799 (ill.)

Black and rufous sengis, *M 5:* 1225

Black and white dwarf boas, *R 2:* 369

Black-and-white warblers, *B 5:* 1263–1264, 1263 (ill.), 1264 (ill.)

Black bears
    American, *M 3:* 593, 596–598, 596 (ill.), 597 (ill.)
    Asiatic, *M 3:* 593, 594, 595

Black-bellied dippers, *B 4:* 1010

Black-bellied hamsters, *M 5:* 1058–1059, 1058 (ill.), 1059 (ill.)

Black-bellied plovers, *B 2:* 446

Black-belted flowerpeckers, *B 5:* 1196

Black-billed wood ducks, *B 2:* 259

Black-breasted buttonquails, *B 2:* 328

Black bulbuls, *B 4:* 945, 952–953, 952 (ill.), 953 (ill.)

Black caimans, *R 1:* 116

Black-capped chickadees, *B 5:* 1167–1169, 1167 (ill.), 1168 (ill.)

Black-capped donacobius, *B 4:* 1047–1049, 1047 (ill.), 1048 (ill.)

Black-capped vireos, *B 5:* 1238–1240, 1238 (ill.), 1239 (ill.)

Black catbirds, *B 4:* 998

Black-cinnamon fantails, *B 4:* 1105

Black corals, *CJ* 39–40, 39 (ill.), 40 (ill.)

Black crested gibbons, *M 3:* 552

Black-crowned barwings, *B 4:* 1028–1029, 1028 (ill.), 1029 (ill.)

Black cuckoos. *See* Anis

Black Death, *M 5:* 1000

Black eels. *See* Cayenne caecilians

Black-eyed frogs, *A 2:* 261–262

Black-faced lion tamarins, *M 3:* 497

Black-faced sheathbills, *B 2:* 469, 472–473, 472 (ill.), 473 (ill.)

Black finless dolphins, *M 4:* 715

Black flies, *I 2:* 338, 340

Black-footed ferrets, *M 3:* 581, 614, 615

Black guans, *B 2:* 284–285, 284 (ill.), 285 (ill.)

Black-headed bushmasters, *R 2:* 390–391, 390 (ill.), 391 (ill.)

Black-headed nasute termites, *I 1:* 128–129, 128 (ill.), 129 (ill.)

Black-headed pythons, *R 2:* 356–357, 356 (ill.), 357 (ill.)

Black-headed weavers. *See* Village weavers

Black herons, *B 1:* 150

Black lampshells, *CM* 320–321, 320 (ill.), 321 (ill.)

Black larks, *B 4:* 903

Black-legged seriemas, *B 2:* 383

Black lemurs, *M 3:* 424

Black lion tamarins, *M 3:* 497

Black-lipped pearl oysters, *CM* 277–278, 277 (ill.), 278 (ill.)

Black macrotermes, *I 1:* 126–127, 126 (ill.), 127 (ill.)

Black mastiff bats, *M 2:* 401

Black-naped monarchs, *B 5:* 1120–1122, 1120 (ill.), 1121 (ill.)

Black-necked cranes, *B 2:* 319

Black-necked spitting cobras, *R 2:* 419–420, 419 (ill.), 420 (ill.)

Black pillows. *See* Black-naped monarchs

Black porpoises. *See* Burmeister's porpoises

Black rails, *B 2:* 356, 362 (ill.), 363, 363 (ill.)

Black rats, *M 5:* 1000

Black rhinoceroses, *M 4:* 850, 874, 876

Black sicklebills, *B 5:* 1390

Black-spotted cuscuses, *M 1:* 116, 117, 118

Black squirrel monkeys, *M 3:* 488

Black stilts, *B 2:* 424, 425

Black storks, *B 1:* 166

Black-tailed hutias, *M 5:* 1188

Black-tailed native-hens, *B 2:* 358

Black-tailed prairie dogs, *M 5:* 1015–1016, 1015 (ill.), 1016 (ill.)

Black-tailed treecreepers, *B 5:* 1147

Black terns, *B 2:* 483–484, 483 (ill.), 484 (ill.)

Black tinamous, *B 1:* 7

Black vultures, *B 1:* 175

Black widow spiders, European, *CM* 176

Black wildebeest, *M 4:* 976–977, 976 (ill.), 977 (ill.)

Black-winged stilts, *B 2:* 424, 425, 426–427, 426 (ill.), 427 (ill.)

Black woodpeckers, *B 3:* 728

Blackbar soldierfishes, *F* 227–228, 227 (ill.), 228 (ill.)

Blackbirds, New World, *B 4:* 1013, *B 5:* **1268–1277**

Blackfin pearl killifishes, *F* 216–217, 216 (ill.), 217 (ill.)

Blackfishes. *See* Bowfins

Blackish blind snakes, *R 2:* 306–307, 306 (ill.), 307 (ill.)

Blackish shrew opossums, *M 1:* 38–39

Blatta orientalis. See Oriental cockroaches

Blattella germanica. See German cockroaches

Blattodea. *See* Cockroaches

Blennies, F 299–304

Blennioidei. *See* Blennies

Blind lizards. *See* Blindskinks

Blind river dolphins. *See* Ganges dolphins; Indus dolphins

Blind sand burrowers. *See* Marsupial moles

Blind skinks. *See* Blindskinks

Blind snakes, *R 1:* 140, *R 2:* 288–289, 295, **302–308**, 337
   early, *R 2:* **288–294**, 295
   false, *R 2:* **309–313,** 312 (ill.), 313 (ill.), 320
   slender, *R 1:* 140, *R 2:* 288–289, **295–301,** 402

Blindskinks, *R 1:* **186–189,** 188 (ill.), 189 (ill.), *R 2:* 260, 262

Blister beetles, *I 2:* 294, 295

Blood-feeding leeches, *CM* 26

Blood-sucking parasites, *CM* 205

Blood worms, *I 2:* 339

Bloodsucker agamids, Indian, *R 1:* 147

Bloody Bay poison frogs, *A 2:* 224

Blubber, *M 4:* 768

Blue-back frogs. *See* Madagascar reed frogs

Blue-bellied poison frogs, *A 2:* 220, 222–223

Blue birds of paradise, *B 5:* 1390

Blue-black grassquits, *B 5:* 1253–1254, 1253 (ill.), 1254 (ill.)

Blue bustards, *B 2:* 392–394, 392 (ill.), 393 (ill.)

Blue cranes, *B 2:* 319

Blue-crowned motmots, *B 3:* 679–681, 679 (ill.), 680 (ill.)

Blue fairies of the forest. *See* Black-naped monarchs

Blue-footed boobies, *B 1:* 130–131, 130 (ill.), 131 (ill.)

Blue-gray gnatcatchers, *B 4:* 1051, 1055–1057, 1055 (ill.), 1056 (ill.)

Blue-headed picathartes. *See* Gray-necked picathartes

Blue jays, *B 5:* 1398, 1401–1402, 1401 (ill.), 1402 (ill.)

Blue marlins, *F* 336–337, 336 (ill.), 337 (ill.)

Blue monkeys, *M 3:* 424

Blue morphos, *I 2:* 381–382, 381 (ill.), 382 (ill.)

Blue-naped mousebirds, *B 3:* 639

Blue spiny lizards, *R 1:* 169

Blue starfishes, *CJ* 194–195, 194 (ill.), 195 (ill.)

Blue swallows, *B 4:* 915

Blue-throated motmots, *B 3:* 677

Blue-toed rocket frogs, *A 2:* 222–223, 232–234, 232 (ill.), 233 (ill.)

Blue toucans, *B 3:* 728, 759

Blue vangas, *B 4:* 972, 973

Blue wattled crows. *See* Kokakos

Blue whales, *CM* 112, *M 4:* 796, 797, 798–799, 798 (ill.), 799 (ill.)

Bluebirds
   eastern, *B 4:* 1017–1019, 1017 (ill.), 1018 (ill.)
   fairy, *B 4:* **955–961**

Bluefin tunas, *F* 335, 338–339, 338 (ill.), 339 (ill.)

Bluegills, *F* 256

Bluestreak cleaner wrasses, *F* 275–276, 275 (ill.), 276 (ill.)

Bluetail mole skinks, *R 2:* 252

Boa constrictors, *R 1:* 141, 142, *R 2:* 342–343, 346–347, 346 (ill.), 347 (ill.)

Boarfishes, red, *F* 231–232, 231 (ill.), 232 (ill.)

Boas, *R 2:* **342–352**, 353, 369, 370

    See also Neotropical sunbeam snakes; Splitjaw snakes

Boat-billed herons, *B 1:* 149

Bobcats, *M 3:* 670–672, 670 (ill.), 671 (ill.)

Bobtail skinks, *R 2:* 250–251

Bobwhites, *B 2:* 303, 304

    masked, *B 2:* 308

    northern, *B 2:* 306–308, 306 (ill.), 307 (ill.)

Body lice, *I 2:* 231–233, 231 (ill.), 232 (ill.)

Body part regrowth. *See* Regeneration

Bog turtles, small, *R 1:* 50

Boidae. *See* Boas

Bolburn's tuco-tucos, *M 5:* 1167

Bolitoglossa pesrubra. See Talamancan web-footed salamanders

Bolivian bleating frogs, *A 3:* 370, 373–374

Bolivian chinchilla rats, *M 5:* 1178

Bolyeriidae. *See* Splitjaw snakes

Bombardier beetles, *I 2:* 294

Bombina bombina. See Fire-bellied toads

Bombina orientalis. See Oriental fire-bellied toads

Bombina variegata. See Yellow-bellied toads

Bombinatoridae. *See* Barbourulas; Fire-bellied toads

Bombycilla cedrorum. See Cedar waxwings

Bombycillidae. *See* Silky flycatchers; Waxwings

Bombyx mori. See Silkworms

Bonaparte's nightjars, *B 3:* 577, 604

Bonefishes, F 55–59, 57 (ill.), 58 (ill.)

Bonellia viridis. See Green bonellias

Bonellin, *CM* 52

Bonobos, *M 3:* 563, 564

Bony tongues, F 46–49

Boobies, *B 1:* 99, 100, 125–133

Book lice, *I 2:* 222–226, 225 (ill.), 226 (ill.)

Book scorpions, *I 1:* 34–35, 34 (ill.), 35 (ill.)

Boomslangs, *R 2:* 402, 403–404, 403 (ill.), 404 (ill.)

Boreal owls, *B 3:* 565

Bornean bristleheads, *B 5:* 1374, 1375–1376, 1375 (ill.), 1376 (ill.)

Bornean flat-headed frogs, *A 1:* 29

Bornean frogmouths, *B 3:* 587

Bornean orangutans, *M 3:* 425, 565–567, 565 (ill.), 566 (ill.)

Bornean smooth-tailed tree shrews, *M 2:* 265

Borneo tree-hole frogs, *A 3:* 372

Botaurus stellaris. See Eurasian bitterns

Botha's larks, *B 4:* 905

Bothus lunatus. See Peacock flounders

Botia macraecanthus. See Clown loaches

Botos, *M 4:* 724–728, 726 (ill.), 727 (ill.)

Botryllus schlosseri, *CJ* 253–254, 253 (ill.), 254 (ill.)

Botta's pocket gophers. *See* Valley pocket gophers

Bottle flies, *I 2:* 340

Bottleheads. *See* Northern bottlenosed whales

Bottlenosed dolphins, *M 4:* 717, 744–745, 744 (ill.), 745 (ill.)

Bottlenosed whales, *M 4:* 751, 752–754, 752 (ill.), 753 (ill.)

Bottom-feeding fishes, *F* 85

Boubous, *B 4:* 963

Bougainville's skinks, *R 2:* 251

Boulenger's callulops frogs, *A 3:* 369, 371, 372

Boulenger's climbing frogs, *A 3:* 372–374

Bovidae. *See* Antelopes; Bison; Buffaloes; Cattle; Goats; Sheep

Bowerbirds, *B 5:* 1146, 1380–1388

Bowfins, F 41–45, 43 (ill.), 44 (ill.)

Bowhead whales, *M 4:* 787–794, 790 (ill.), 791 (ill.)

Box jellies, CJ 53–56

Box turtles

    eastern, *R 1:* 55–57, 55 (ill.), 56 (ill.)

    yellow-margined, *R 1:* 61–63, 61 (ill.), 62 (ill.)

Brachiosaurus species, *R 1:* 1, 2

Brachipoda. *See* Lampshells

Brachycephalidae. *See* Three-toed toadlets

Brachycephalus. See Three-toed toadlets

Brachycephalus didactyla, **A 2:** 192

Brachycephalus ephippium. See Pumpkin toadlets

Brachycephalus nodoterga, **A 2:** 192–193

Brachycephalus pernix, **A 2:** 192–193

Brachycephalus vertebralis, **A 2:** 192–193

Brachytarsophrys intermedia. See Annam broad-headed toads

Bradypodidae. *See* Three-toed tree sloths

Bradypus species, *M 1:* 190

Bradypus variegatus. See Brown throated three-toed sloths

Brahminy blind snakes, *R 2:* 303

Buckler dories, *F* 230

Bucorvus leadbeateri. See Southern ground-hornbills

Budgett's frogs, **A** *2:* 155, 161–163, 161 (ill.), 162 (ill.)

Buenea Vista Lake ornate shrews, *M 2:* 216, 249

Buerger's frogs, **A** *3:* 350, 351, 353–354

Buff-breasted buttonquails, *B 2:* 328

Buff-breasted sandpipers, *B 2:* 455

Buff-spotted flufftails, *B 2:* 360–361, 360 (ill.), 361 (ill.)

Buff-throated purpletufts, *B 4:* 874

Buffalo-weavers, red-billed, *B 5:* 1307, 1308–1309

Buffaloes, *M 4:* **969–987**

Buffy headed marmosets, *M 3:* 497

Buffy tufted-ear marmosets, *M 3:* 497

Bufo marinus. See Marine toads

Bufo periglenes. See Golden toads

Bufonidae. *See* Harlequin frogs; True toads

Bugs, true, *I 2:* **236–256**

Bulbuls, *B 4:* **943–954**

Bulldog bats, *M 2:* **364–370**

Bullfrogs, **A** *1:* 3, **A** *2:* 290, 292, 303–305, 303 (ill.), 304 (ill.)

Bumbleebee bats. *See* Kitti's hog-nosed bats

Buphagus erythrorhynchus. See Red-billed oxpeckers

Bureau of Land Management, *M 4:* 851

Burhinidae. *See* Thick-knees

Buried-eyed caecilians, **A** *3:* **522–526**

Burmeister's porpoises, *M 4:* 730, 731, 734–735, 734 (ill.), 735 (ill.)

Burmese bubble-nest frogs, **A** *3:* 352

Burmese spadefoot toads, **A** *1:* 78

Burramyidae. *See* Pygmy possums

Burrowing asps, *R 2:* 394–395, 396–397, 396 (ill.), 397 (ill.)

Burrowing barnacles, *CM* 198

Burrowing bettongs, *M 1:* 130

Burrowing boas. *See* Neotropical sunbeam snakes

Burrowing frogs, **A** *3:* 371

Burrowing owls, *B 3:* 554, 565

Burrowing pikas, *M 5:* 1201, 1206

Burrowing snakes
  African, *R 2:* **393–398**
  shieldtail, *R 2:* 315

Burrows, nest, *B 2:* 414
  See also specific species

Burying beetles, *I 2:* 293, 296, 310–311, 310 (ill.), 311 (ill.)

Bush crickets, Oahu deceptor, *I 1:* 172

Bush dogs, *M 3:* 583

Bush hyraxes, *M 4:* 821

Bush-shrikes, *B 4:* 962, 963, 964

Bush squeakers, **A** *2:* 311, 313–314

Bush thick-knees, *B 2:* 433

Bushbabies, *M 3:* 423, 424, 425, **436–443**

Bushbirds, Rondonia, *B 4:* 838

Bushlarks, Sidamo, *B 4:* 905

Bushmeat, *M 4:* 889

Bushtits, *B 5:* 1151–1153, 1154–1156, 1154 (ill.), 1155 (ill.)

Bushveld rain frogs, **A** *3:* 369, 370–373

Bustards, *B 2:* 315, 316, 318–319, **387–394**

Busuanga jungle toads. *See* Philippine barbourulas

Butcherbirds, *B 5:* 1372–1374, 1377–1379, 1377 (ill.), 1378 (ill.)

See also Loggerhead shrikes; Shrikes

Butterfishes, F **343–346,** 345 (ill.), 346 (ill.)

Butterflies, *I 2:* **366–389**

Butterflyfishes, freshwater, *F* 48–49, 48 (ill.), 49 (ill.)

Buttonquails, *B 2:* 316, 317, **326–332**

C

Cacajao calvus. See Bald uakaris

Cacklers, red-breasted. *See* Gray-crowned babblers

Cactus wrens, *B 4:* 1037, 1038, 1040–1042, 1040 (ill.), 1041 (ill.)

Caddisflies, *I 1:* 94, *I 2:* **358–365**

Caecilians, **A** *3:* **501–505**
  American tailed, **A** *3:* **506–510**
  Asian tailed, **A** *3:* **511–516**
  buried-eyed, **A** *3:* **522–526**
  tailless, **A** *3:* **527–535**

Caeciliidae. *See* Tailless caecilians

Caenolestes fuliginosus. See Silky shrew opossums

Caenolestidae. *See* Shrew opossums

Cage birds, *B 3:* 523
  See also specific species

Caiman crocodilus. See Common caimans

Caiman lizards, Paraguayan, *R 2:* 236

Caimans, *R 1:* **114–122**

Calabar ground boas, *R 2:* 344

Calcium in eggshells, *B 1:* 72

Caldwell, William Hay, *M 1:* 5

Calfbirds, *B 4:* 874

Cariamidae. *See* Seriemas

Caribbean monk seals, *M 3:* 581, 691

Caribbean spiny lobsters, *CM* 123

Caribou, *M 4:* 951

Carmine dye, *I 2:* 240

Carnassial teeth, *M 3:* 581

Carnivora. *See* Land carnivores; Marine carnivores

Carnivores, land and marine, *M 3:* **578–582**

Carnivorous marsupials, Australasian, *M 1:* **51–55,** 75

Carolina parakeets, *B 3:* 523

Carolina wrens, *B 4:* 1037

Carpenterworms, *I 2:* 372

Carps, F 84–91

Carrion, *B 1:* 176

Carrion beetles, *I 2:* 293

Carrizo Plain Natural Heritage Reserve, *M 5:* 1042

Casarea dussumieri. See Splitjaw snakes

Cascade torrent salamanders, *A 3:* 473–475, 473 (ill.), 474 (ill.)

Casiraguas, *M 5:* 1182

Caspian seals, *M 3:* 691

Cassowaries, *B 1:* 1, 2, 3, **18–23**

Castor canadensis. See North American beavers

Castoridae. *See* Beavers

Casuariidae. *See* Cassowaries

Casuarius bennetti. See Dwarf cassowaries

Casuarius casuarius. See Southern cassowaries

Cat-eyed frogs, *A 1:* 77

Cat fleas, *I 2:* 328, 330

Catbirds, *B 4:* 998, 999–1000, 999 (ill.), 1000 (ill.)

Caterpillars, *I 2:* 372

Catfishes, F 101–108

Cathartidae. *See* New World vultures

Catholic frogs. *See* Crucifix frogs

Cats, *M 3:* 578, 579, 582, **657–672**

domestic, *M 3:* 658

marsupial, *M 1:* **56–63**

wild, *M 3:* 581, 658

Cattle, *M 4:* 890, **969–987**

Cattle egrets, *B 1:* 145, 155–156, 155 (ill.), 156 (ill.)

Caucasian mud-divers. *See* Caucasus parsley frogs

Caucasian parsley frogs. *See* Caucasus parsley frogs

Caucasian salamanders, *A 3:* 443

Caucasus parsley frogs, *A 1:* 102, 103

Caudata. *See* Newts; Salamanders

Cave crickets, *I 1:* 168

Cave squeakers, *A 2:* 314

Cave swiftlets, *B 3:* 613, 616

Caves, anchialine, *CM* 161

Caviar, *F* 33

Cavies, *M 5:* 996, 999, 1000, **1139–1146**

Caviidae. *See* Cavies; Maras

Cavity nesters, *B 4:* 831

See also specific species

Cayenne caecilians, *A 3:* 533–535, 533 (ill.), 534 (ill.)

Cebidae. *See* Capuchins; Squirrel monkeys

Cebuella pygmaea. See Pygmy marmosets

Cebus capucinus. See White-throated capuchins

Cebus olivaceus. See Weeper capuchins

Cedar waxwings, *B 4:* 979–984, 982 (ill.), 983 (ill.)

Cell regrowth. *See* Regeneration

Cellar spiders, long-bodied, *I 1:* 32–33, 32 (ill.), 33 (ill.)

Centipede eaters, *R 2:* 394, 395

Centipedes, *I 2:* **415–424**

Central American agoutis, *M 5:* 1156–1158, 1156 (ill.), 1157 (ill.)

Central American river turtles, *R 1:* **39–43,** 41 (ill.), 42 (ill.)

Central valley grasshoppers, *I 1:* 171

Centrolene ballux, **A** *2:* 248

Centrolene buckleyi, **A** *2:* 244

Centrolene geckoideum. See Pacific giant glass frogs

Centrolene gemmatum, **A** *2:* 248

Centrolene heloderma, **A** *2:* 248–249

Centrolene puyoense, **A** *2:* 248–249

Centrolenidae. *See* Glass frogs

Cephalaspidomorphi. *See* Lampreys

Cephalocarida. *See* Cephalocarids

Cephalocarids, CM 71–74

Cephalochordata. *See* Lancelets

Cephalopoda, CM 293–305

Cephalopterus ornatus. See Amazonian umbrellabirds

Cerastes cerastes. See Horned vipers

Ceratophrys cornuta. See Surinam horned frogs

Ceratosaurus species, *R 1:* 1

Ceratotherium simum. See White rhinoceroses

Cercartetus nanus. See Eastern pygmy possums

Cercomacra cinerascens. See Gray antbirds

Cercopithecidae. *See* Old World monkeys

Certhia americana. See Brown creepers

Certhiidae. *See* Treecreepers

Cervidae. *See* Deer

Cervus elaphus. See Red deer

Cestum veneris. See Sea walnuts; Venus's girdles

Chinese ferret badgers, *M 3:* 629

Chinese giant salamanders, **A** *3:* 419–420

Chinese mantids, *I 1:* 149–150, 149 (ill.), 150 (ill.)

Chinese river dolphins. *See* Baijis

Chinese salamanders, **A** *3:* 410

Chinese stripe-necked turtles, *R 1:* 59

Chinook salmons, *F* 129–130, 129 (ill.), 130 (ill.)

Chioglossa lusitanica. See Golden-striped salamanders

Chionidae. *See* Sheathbills

Chionis minor. See Black-faced sheathbills

Chipmunks, *M 5:* 996, 1009
   American, *M 5:* 1008
   eastern, *M 5:* 1013–1014, 1013 (ill.), 1014 (ill.)

Chiricahua leopard frogs, **A** *2:* 292

Chiridotea caeca. See Sand isopods

Chirinda toads, **A** *2:* 199

Chironectes minimus. See Water opossums

Chironex fleckeri. See Sea wasps

Chiroptera. *See* Bats

Chiroxiphia linearis. See Long-tailed manakins

Chitin, *CM* 33

Chitons, CM 252–259

Chlamydera maculata. See Spotted bowerbirds

Chlamydosaurus kingii. See Frilled lizards

Chlamyphorus truncatus. See Pink fairy armadillos

Chlamys opercularis. See Queen scallops

Chlidonias niger. See Black terns

Choco tinamous, *B 1:* 7

Choloepus. See Two-toed tree sloths

Choloepus hoffmanni. See Hoffmann's two-toed sloths

Chondrichthyes. *See* Chimaeras; Rays; Sharks; Skates

Chordates, *CJ* 249

Choughs, white-winged, *B 5:* 1360

Chowchillas, B 4: 1093–1098

Christmas frigatebirds, *B 1:* 110

Christmas Island blind snakes, *R 2:* 305

Chrysaora quinquecirrha. See Sea nettles

Chrysemys picta. See Painted turtles

Chrysochloridae. *See* Golden moles

Chrysocyon brachyurus. See Maned wolves

Chrysomyia species. *See* Latrine flies

Chubby frogs. *See* Malaysian painted frogs

Chuckwallas, common, *R 1:* 168, 172–173, 172 (ill.), 173 (ill.)

Chytrid fungus, **A** *1:* 4, 11, **A** *2:* 203, 210, 216, 224 -225, 249, 264, 292

Cicadas, I 2: 236–256

Cichlids, F 272–280

Cicinnurus regius. See King birds of paradise

Ciconia ciconia. See European white storks

Ciconiidae. *See* Storks

Ciconiiformes, B 1: 143–148

Ciguetera poison, *F* 260

Cimex lectularius. See Bed bugs

Cinclidae. *See* Dippers

Cinclosoma punctatum. See Spotted quail-thrushes

Cinclus cinclus. See Eurasian dippers

Cinclus mexicanus. See American dippers

Cinerous wattled birds. *See* Kokakos

Cinnamon-tailed fantails, *B 4:* 1109

Cinnamon treefrogs. *See* Painted Indonesian treefrogs

Cinnyris asiaticus. See Purple sunbirds

Cissa chinensis. See Green magpies

Cisticola juncidis. See Zitting cisticolas

Cisticolas, zitting, *B 4:* 1053–1054, 1053 (ill.), 1054 (ill.)

Cistoclemmys flavomarginata. See Yellow-margined box turtles

CITES (Convention on International Trade in Endangered Species), *R 2:* 338, 340
   on eclectus parrots, *B 3:* 528
   on emperor scorpions, *I 1:* 44
   on giant birdwing butterflies, *I 2:* 372–373
   on helmeted hornbills, *B 3:* 721
   United Nations stamps, *M 1:* 117

Civets, M 3: 579, 580–582, **628–636**

Civettictis civetta. See African civets

Clam shrimps, CM 75–86

Clam worms, CM 1–11

Clams, **CM 276**
   coquina, *CM* 282–283, 282 (ill.), 283 (ill.)
   geoducks, *CM* 275
   giant, *CM* 276, 286–287, 286 (ill.), 287 (ill.)
   lampshells and, *CM* 319

Clarion wrens, *B 4:* 1039

Common bulbuls, *B 4:* 938
(ill.), 943, 944, 947–949, 947
(ill.)

Common buttonquails, *B 2:* 328

Common caimans, *R 1:*
120–121, 120 (ill.), 121 (ill.)

Common chameleons, *R 1:*
164–165, 164 (ill.), 165 (ill.)

Common chuckwallas, *R 1:*
168, 172–173, 172 (ill.), 173
(ill.)

Common cuckoos, *B 3:* 545,
547–548, 547 (ill.), 548 (ill.),
B 4: 1061

Common diving-petrels, *B 1:*
67, 68, 69–70, 69 (ill.), 70
(ill.)

Common dolphinfishes, *F*
263–264, 263 (ill.), 264 (ill.)

Common garter snakes, *R 2:*
400, 405–406, 405 (ill.), 406
(ill.)

Common genets, *M 3:*
634–636, 634 (ill.), 635 (ill.)

Common harvestman, *I 1:* 15,
27–28, 27 (ill.), 28 (ill.)

Common hippopotamuses, *M
4:* 909, 910–912, 910 (ill.),
911 (ill.)

Common ioras, *B 4:* 956,
958–959, 958 (ill.), 959 (ill.)

Common long-nosed
armadillos. *See* Nine-banded
armadillos

Common loons, *B 1:* 87–89,
87 (ill.), 88 (ill.)

Common mealworm, *I 2:* 298

Common mouse opossums, *M
1:* 28

Common murres, *B 2:*
489–491, 489 (ill.), 490 (ill.)

Common musk turtles. *See*
Stinkpots

Common mynas, *B 5:*
1329–1330, 1329 (ill.), 1330
(ill.)

Common octopuses, *CM*
301–302, 301 (ill.), 302 (ill.)

Common opossums. *See*
Virginia opossums

Common parsley frogs. *See*
Parsley frogs

Common pill woodlice, *CM*
178–179, 178 (ill.), 179
(ill.)

Common plantannas, *A 1:* 64,
65, 67–69, 67 (ill.), 68 (ill.)

Common potoos. *See* Gray
potoos

Common redshanks, *B 2:* 454

Common reed frogs. *See*
Painted reed frogs

Common ringtails, *M 1:*
159–160, 159 (ill.), 160 (ill.)

Common shiny woodlice, *CM*
182–183, 182 (ill.), 183 (ill.)

Common slit-faced bats. *See*
Egyptian slit-faced bats

Common snake-necked turtles,
R 1: 19

Common sole, *F* 363–364, 363
(ill.), 364 (ill.)

Common spadefoot frogs, *A 1:*
127

Common spotted cuscuses, *M
1:* 117, 118

Common squeakers, *A 2:*
310–311, 313, 316–318, 316
(ill.), 317 (ill.)

Common squirrel monkeys, *M
3:* 489–490, 489 (ill.), 490
(ill.)

Common sunbeam snakes, *R
2:* 331, 334–335, 334 (ill.),
335 (ill.)

Common sunbird-asities, *B 4:*
801, 802, 803, 804–805, 804
(ill.), 805 (ill.)

Common tenrecs, *M 2:* 232,
235–236, 235 (ill.), 236 (ill.)

Common tree shrews, *M 2:*
266–268, 266 (ill.), 267 (ill.)

Common treefrogs, *A 3:* 353,
355

Common trumpeters, *B 2:*
379–381, 379 (ill.), 380 (ill.)

Common water fleas, *CM*
84–85, 84 (ill.), 85 (ill.)

Common waxbills, *B 5:*
1299–1300, 1299 (ill.), 1300
(ill.)

Common wombats, *M 1:* 102,
111, 114–115, 114 (ill.), 115
(ill.)

Commonwealth of the
Northern Mariana Islands
(CNMI), *M 2:* 286–287

Communal breeding, *B 5:*
1140

    See also specific species

Communication, dolphin, *M 4:*
739

Concentricycloidea. *See* Sea
daisies

Condors, *B 1:* 143, 146, 175,
176

    Andean, *B 1:* 177

    California, *B 1:* 147, 177,
    181–182, 181 (ill.), 182
    (ill.)

Condylura cristata. See Star-
nosed moles

Cone shells, geography, *CM*
272–273, 272 (ill.), **273**
(ill.)

Coneheads, long-winged, *I 1:*
181–182, 181 (ill.), 182
(ill.)

Conejo pintados. *See* Pacas

Congo bay owls, *B 3:* 565

Congo eels. *See* Amphiumas

Congo snakes. *See* Amphiumas

Congo swifts, *B 3:* 617

Connochaetes gnou. See Black
wildebeest

Conocephalus discolor. See
Long-winged coneheads

Conondale gastric brooding
frogs. *See* Northern gastric
brooding frogs

Conraua goliath. See Goliath
frogs

Conus geographus. See
Geography cone shells

Cracticus torquatus. See Gray butcherbirds

Crag martins, *B 4:* 922–923, 922 (ill.), 923 (ill.)

Crane flies, European marsh, *I 2:* 355–356, 355 (ill.), 356 (ill.)

Cranes, *B 2:* 315–319, **333–343,** 345

Craseonycteridae. *See* Kitti's hog-nosed bats

Craseonycteris thonglongyai. See Kitti's hog-nosed bats

Crax globulosa. See Wattled curassows

Crayfishes, *CM* 121–137, 233

Crazy widows. *See* Limpkins

Creepers

　Australian, *B 5:* **1145–1150**

　brown, *B 5:* 1184–1185, 1184 (ill.), 1185 (ill.)

　Hawaiian honeycreepers, *B 5:* 1209, **1288–1295**

　Philippine, *B 5:* **1188–1193**

　treecreepers, *B 5:* **1182–1187,** 1189

　wall, *B 5:* **1173–1181**

　woodcreepers, *B 4:* **830–835**

Crepuscular birds, *B 2:* 432

　See also specific species

Crested bellbirds, *B 5:* 1131, 1132

Crested berrypeckers, *B 5:* 1196

Crested capuchins, *M 3:* 488

Crested caracaras, *B 1:* 231–233, 231 (ill.), 232 (ill.)

Crested genets, *M 3:* 629

Crested guineafowl, *B 2:* 289

Crested larks, *B 4:* 901, 903

Crested porcupines

　Indian, *M 5:* 1115–1116, 1115 (ill.), 1116 (ill.)

　North African, *M 5:* 1114

Crested swifts. *See* Tree swifts

Crested tinamous, *B 1:* 7

Crested tree swifts, *B 3:* 624, 625, 627–629, 627 (ill.), 628 (ill.)

Crex crex. See Corncrakes

Cribellate spiders, *I 1:* 17

Cricetomys gambianus. See Gambian rats

Cricetus cricetus. See Black-bellied hamsters

Cricket frogs, *A 2:* **310–322**

Crickets, *I 1:* 158, **166–187**

Crimson chats, *B 4:* 1087, 1088, 1089, 1090–1092, 1090 (ill.), 1091 (ill.)

Crinoidea. *See* Feather stars; Sea lilies

Crocodile lizards, Chinese, *R 2:* 268, 269

Crocodile monitors, *R 1:* 140, *R 2:* 279, 285–286, 285 (ill.), 286 (ill.)

Crocodile tegus, *R 2:* 240–241, 240 (ill.), 241 (ill.)

Crocodiles, *R 1:* 2, 101–107, **123–131**

Crocodilians, *R 1:* **101–107**

Crocodilurus lacertinus. See Crocodile tegus

Crocodylidae. *See* Crocodiles; False gharials

Crocodylus acutus. See American crocodiles

Crocodylus niloticus. See Nile crocodiles

Crocuta crocuta. See Spotted hyenas

Crop milk, *B 3:* 506, 509

Cropan's boas, *R 2:* 345

Crossbills, *B 4:* 790, *B 5:* 1285–1287, 1285 (ill.), 1286 (ill.)

Crotalus horridus. See Timber rattlesnakes

Crown-of-thorns, *CJ* 192–193, 192 (ill.), 193 (ill.)

Crowned forest frogs, *A 2:* 310–311, 311

Crowned lemurs, *M 3:* 455–457, 455 (ill.), 456 (ill.)

Crowned poison frogs. *See* Red-headed poison frogs

Crows, *B 4:* 789, *B 5:* 1119, **1398–1410**

　See also Gray-necked picathartes; Kokakos

Crucifix frogs, *A 1:* 124

Cryptobiosis, *CM* 62, 63

Cryptobranchidae. *See* Asiatic giant salamanders; Hellbenders

Cryptobranchus alleganiensis. See Hellbenders

Cryptochiton stelleri. See Gumboot chitons

Cryptodira, *R 1:* 9, 14

Cryptomys damarensis. See Damaraland mole-rats

Cryptoprocta ferox. See Fossa

Cryptoprocta spelea, M 3: 646

Cryptotis parva. See American least shrews

Ctenodactylidae. *See* Gundis

Ctenomyidae. *See* Tuco-tucos

Ctenomys pearsoni. See Pearson's tuco-tucos

Ctenophora. *See* Comb jellies

Ctenosaura hemilopha. See Cape spinytail iguanas

Cubacubana spelaea, I 1: 69–70, 69 (ill.), 70 (ill.)

Cuban black and white dwarf boas, *R 2:* 369

Cuban cranes, *B 2:* 340

Cuban dusky tropes, *R 2:* 369

Cuban hutias, *M 5:* 1188, 1189, 1191–1193, 1191 (ill.), 1192 (ill.)

Cuban Iberian rain frogs, *A 1:* 1

Cuban night lizards, *R 2:* 216, 217

Cuban solenodons, *M 2:* 240, 242

Cuban todies, *B 3:* 669, 673–674, 673 (ill.), 674 (ill.)

Cubozoa. *See* Box jellies

Cuckoo bees, *I 2:* 393

Cuckoo finches, *B 5:* 1308

Cuckoo rollers, *B 3:* 691, 692, 693

Cuckoo-shrikes, *B 4:* **935–942**

Cuckoos, *B 3:* **545–551,** *B 4:* 1061
    bronze, *B 4:* 1071, 1080, 1089
    dideric, *B 5:* 1312
    pallid, *B 4:* 1108
    See also Anis

Cuculidae. *See* Anis; Cuckoos; Roadrunners

Cuculiformes. *See* Anis; Cuckoos; Roadrunners

Cuculus canorus. See Common cuckoos

Cucumbers, sea, *CM* 243

Cumacea. *See* Cumaceans

Cumaceans, *CM* 150–154

Cuniculus brisson. See Pacas

Curassows, *B 2:* 267, **279–287**

Curlews, *B 2:* 454
    bristle-thighed, *B 2:* 456
    eskimo, *B 2:* 397, 456
    long-billed, *B 2:* 459–460, 459 (ill.), 460 (ill.)
    slender-billed, *B 2:* 456
    stone, *B 2:* 432, 433

Currawongs, *B 4:* 1108, *B 5:* 1372–1374

Cururo lesser escuerzos, *A 2:* 156

Cururu toads. *See* Rococo toads

Cuscomys ashaninki, M 5: 1178

Cuscomys oblativa, M 5: 1178

Cuscuses, *M 1:* 99, **116–123**

Cusk-eels, *F* **167–172**

Cuttlefishes, *CM* **293–305**

Cutworms, *I 2:* 372

Cuvier's dwarf caimans, *R 1:* 102, 114

Cuvier's whales, *M 4:* 751

Cyanocitta cristata. See Blue jays

Cyclarhis gujanensis. See Rufous-browed peppershrikes

Cyclaspis longicaudata, CM 153–154, 153 (ill.), 154 (ill.)

Cycliophora. *See* Wheel wearers

Cyclopes didactylus. See Silky anteaters

Cyclorana platycephala. See Water-holding frogs

Cygnets, *B 2:* 250

Cygnus olor. See Mute swans

Cylindrophiidae. *See* Pipe snakes

Cylindrophis ruffus. See Red-tailed pipe snakes

Cymbirhynchus macrorhynchos. See Black-and-red broadbills

Cynocephalidae. *See* Colugos

Cynocephalus variegatus. See Malayan colugos

Cynomys ludovicianus. See Black-tailed prairie dogs

Cynops pyrrhogaster. See Japanese fire-bellied newts

Cypress trouts. *See* Bowfins

Cypriniformes, *F* **84–91**

Cyprinodontiformes. *See* Killifishes; Live-bearers

Cypsiurus parvus. See African palm swifts

Cyrtodiopsis dalmanni. See Stalk-eyed flies

Cysts, *CM* 78

D

Dabb spiny-tailed lizards, *R 1:* 146

Dacelo novaeguineae. See Laughing kookaburras

Dactylogyrus vastator, CJ 99–100, 99 (ill.), 100 (ill.)

Dactylopsilinae. *See* Striped possums

Dactyloptena orientalis. See Oriental helmet gurnards

Daddy longlegs. *See* Common harvestman

Dahlella caldariensis, CM 89–90, 89 (ill.), 90 (ill.)

d'Albertis's ringtail possums, *M 1:* 156

Dall's porpoises, *M 4:* 729–730

Dalmation pelicans, *B 1:* 135

Damaraland mole-rats, *M 5:* 1106–1107, 1106 (ill.), 1107 (ill.)

Damselfishes, *F* 272–274

Damselflies, *I 1:* **81–91**

Dance flies, *I 2:* 339

Dance of death, *M 3:* 615

Dandruff, mechanized. *See* Head lice

Danger, to frogs, *A 1:* 4

Daphnia pulex. See Common water fleas

Dark-rumped swifts, *B 3:* 617

Darkling beetles, *I 2:* 291

Darters, *F* **259–271**

Darwin, Charles
    burrowing barnacles, *CM* 198
    earthworms, *CM* 19

Darwin's finches, *R 1:* 88

Darwin's frogs, *A 2:* 182–189, 186 (ill.), 187 (ill.)

Dasprocta species, *M 5:* 1153

Dassie rats, *M 5:* **1093–1096,** 1094 (ill.), 1095 (ill.)

Dasypodidae. *See* Armadillos

Dasyprocta punctata. See Central American agoutis

Dasyproctidae. *See* Agoutis

Dasypus novemcinctus. See Nine-banded armadillos

Dasyuridae. *See* Marsupial cats; Marsupial mice; Tasmanian devils

Dasyuromorphia. *See* Australasian carnivorous marsupials

Douc langurs, red-shanked, *M 3*: 537, 544–545, 544 (ill.), 545 (ill.)

Dourocoulis, *M 3*: 425

Dovekies, *B 2*: 486, 487

Doves, *B 3*: 504–507, **508–516**

Draco volans. See Flying lizards

Dracula (Stoker), *M 2*: 279, 346

Dracunculus mediensis, CM 222

Dragon lizards, *R 1*: 140, **145–155**

Dragonets, *F* **313–316**

Dragonfishes, *F* **136–141**

Dragonflies, *I 1*: **81–91**

Dreissena polymorpha. See Zebra mussels

Drepanididae. *See* Hawaiian honeycreepers

Drepanorhynchus reichenowi. See Golden-winged sunbirds

Dromadidae. *See* Crab plovers

Dromaeosaurids, *R 1*: 6

Dromaiidae. *See* Emus

Dromaius novaehollandiae. See Emus

Dromas ardeola. See Crab plovers

Dromedary camels, *M 4*: 917, 919–920, 919 (ill.), 920 (ill.)

Dromiciops australis. See Monitos del monte

Dromiciops gliroides. See Monitos del monte

Drone flies, *I 2*: 337

Drongos, *B 5*: **1345–1352**

Droppings and diet, *R 1: 198*

Drosophila melanogaster. See Fruit flies

Dryland mouse opossums, *M 1*: 25

Drymarchon corais. See Indigo snakes

Drymodes brunneopygia. See Southern scrub robins

Duck-billed platypus, *M 1*: 1–6, **15–23**, 20 (ill.), 21 (ill.)

Ducks, *B 2*: 241–245, **246–260**

Duets, antiphonal, *B 5*: 1361

Dugesia tigrina. See Freshwater planarians

Dugong dugon. See Dugongs

Dugongidae. *See* Dugongs; Sea cows

Dugongs, *M 4*: 828–832, **833–840**, 838 (ill.), 839 (ill.)

Dulidae. *See* Palmchats

Dulus dominicus. See Palmchats

Dumbacher, Jack, *B 5*: 1132

Dumetella carolinensis. See Gray catbirds

Dune squeakers. *See* Common squeakers

Dung beetles, *I 2*: 293, 296

Dung scarabs, *I 2*: 297, 298

Dunnarts, *M 1*: 54, 58

Dunnocks, *B 4*: 993, 994–996, 994 (ill.), 995 (ill.)

Dupont's larks, *B 4*: 903

Duprat, Hubert, *I 2*: 361

Dusky dwarf boas, *R 2*: 370

Dusky gopher frogs, *A 2*: 292

Dusky salamanders, *A 3*: 479–481, 479 (ill.), 480 (ill.)

Dusky tropes, Cuban, *R 2*: 369

Dusky woodswallows, *B 5*: 1369–1371, 1369 (ill.), 1370 (ill.)

Dustywings, *I 2*: 274, 275

Dwarf boas
    Cuban black and white, *R 2*: 369
    dusky, *R 2*: 370
    Oaxacan, *R 2*: 369
    Panamanian, *R 2*: 370

Dwarf brittle stars, *CJ* 207–208, 207 (ill.), 208 (ill.)

Dwarf cassowaries, *B 1*: 19, 20

Dwarf clawed frogs, *A 1*: 64

Dwarf epauletted fruit bats, *M 2*: 293–294, 293 (ill.), 294 (ill.)

Dwarf geckos. *See* Jaragua lizards

Dwarf gobies, *F* 318

Dwarf gymnures, *M 2*: 220

Dwarf honeyguides, *B 3*: 768

Dwarf lemurs, *M 3*: **444–449**

Dwarf litter frogs, *A 1*: 77

Dwarf mongooses, *M 3*: 638

Dwarf pipe snakes. *See* False blind snakes

Dwarf puff adders, *R 2*: 380

Dwarf pythons. *See* Neotropical sunbeam snakes

Dwarf sirens, *A 3*: **403–408**

Dwarf tinamous, *B 1*: 7

Dynastes hercules. See Hercules beetles

Dytiscus marginalis. See Great water beetles

E

Eagle-owls, *B 3*: 553, 565, 570–571, 570 (ill.), 571 (ill.)

Eagles, *B 1*: 207, 208, 209, **212–222**, *B 2*: 295

Eagles, Philippine, *M 2*: 270

Eared doves, *B 3*: 505

Eared hutias, *M 5*: 1189

Eared seals, *M 3*: 579, 582, **673–683**, 690

Earless monitors, *R 2*: **279–287**

Earless seals. *See* True seals

Early blind snakes, *R 2*: **288–294**, 295

Ears of reptiles, *R 1*: 209

Earth-boring beetles, *I 2*: 296

Earth pigs. *See* Aardvarks

Earthworms, *CM* **17–24**, *R 1*: 191

Earwigflies, *I 2*: 320, 322

Earwigs, *I 1*: **158–165**

Eastern barred bandicoots, *M 1*: 80, 83–84, 83 (ill.), 84 (ill.)

Eastern black gibbons, *M 3*: 552

Eastern bluebirds, *B 4*: 1017–1019, 1017 (ill.), 1018 (ill.)

Eigenmannia lineata. See Glass knifefishes

El Hamma, Tunisia, *CM* 171

Elapidae, *R 2:* **414–426**

Electra pilosa. See Sea mats

Electric eels, F 109–115, 111 (ill.), 112 (ill.)

Electrophorus electricus. See Electric eels

Electroreceptors, *M 1:* 4, 19

Elegant crested tinamous. *See* Crested tinamous

Elegant water shrews, *M 2:* 248

Elephant birds, *B 1:* 3

Elephant seals, *M 3:* 578, 684, 691, 695–697, 695 (ill.), 696 (ill.)

Elephant shrews. *See* Sengis

Elephant-trunk snakes. *See* File snakes

Elephantfishes, *F* 47

Elephantidae. *See* Elephants

Elephantnose fishes, *F* 47

Elephants, *M 4:* **808–819,** 821, 885

Elephas maximus. See Asian elephants

Elf owls, *B 3:* 553

Ellis's sandpipers, *B 2:* 456

Elopiformes. *See* Ladyfishes; Tarpons

Emballonuridae. *See* Ghost bats; Sac-winged bats; Sheath-tailed bats

Emberizidae. *See* New World finches

Embioptera. *See* Webspinners

Emerald notothens, *F* 290–291, 290 (ill.), 291 (ill.)

Emerald toucanets, *B 3:* 759

Emerald tree boas, *R 2:* 348–349, 348 (ill.), 349 (ill.)

Emotions, in elephants, *M 4:* 811

Emperor birds of paradise, *B 5:* 1390

Emperor of the flesh-eating crocodiles, *R 1:* 103

Emperor penguins, *B 1:* 74–76, 74 (ill.), 75 (ill.)

Emperor scorpions, *I 1:* 42–44, 42 (ill.), 43 (ill.)

Emu-wrens, *B 4:* 1070

Emus, *B 1:* 1, 2, 3, **24–28,** 26 (ill.), 27 (ill.)

Emydidae. *See* New World pond turtles

Endangered species, *A 1:* 4, *R 2:* 238

    See also World Conservation Union (IUCN) Red List of Threatened Species; specific species

Endangered Species Act (U.S.)
    black-capped vireos, *B 5:* 1240
    gray wolves, *M 3:* 587
    kagus, *B 2:* 353
    owls, *B 3:* 555
    red-cockaded woodpeckers, *B 3:* 783
    Sirenia, *M 4:* 831

Endemic species, *CM* 166
    See also specific species

Endothermic animals, *R 1:* 2
    See also specific animals

Endoxocrinus parrae. See West Atlantic stalked crinoids

English blind snakes. *See* Blackish blind snakes

English dippers. *See* Eurasian dippers

English Nature Greater Horseshoe Bat Project, *M 2:* 331

Enigmonia species, *CM* 275

Enneapterygius mirabilis. See Miracle triplefins

Enoplans, CJ 112–115

Entropocts, CJ 155–159

Entroprocta. *See* Entropocts

Environmental effects on frogs and toads, *A 1:* 4, *A 2:* 311

See also specific species

Epauletted fruit bats, dwarf, *M 2:* 293–294, 293 (ill.), 294 (ill.)

Ephemera vulgata. See Brown mayflies

Ephemeroptera. *See* Mayflies

Epicrionops marmoratus. See Marbled caecilians

Epinephelus striatus. See Nassau groupers

Epipedobates tricolor. See Phantasmal poison frogs

Epiperipatus biolleyi, CM 59–60, 59 (ill.), 60 (ill.)

Epthianura tricolor. See Crimson chats

Epthianuridae. *See* Australian chats

Equidae. *See* Asses; Horses; Zebras

Equus caballus przewalskii. See Przewalski's horses

Equus grevyi. See Grevy's zebras

Equus kiang. See Kiangs

Erect-crested penguins, *B 1:* 73

Eremitalpa granti. See Grant's desert golden moles

Eremophila alpestris. See Horned larks

Erethizon dorsatum. See North American porcupines

Erethizontidae. *See* New World porcupines

Erie Canal, *F* 6

Erinaceidae. *See* Gymnures; Hedgehogs

Erinaceus europaeus. See Western European hedgehogs

Ermines, *M 3:* 614, 616–618, 616 (ill.), 617 (ill.)

Erythrina polychaeta, CM 4

Esacus magnirostris. See Beach thick-knees

Eschrichtiidae. *See* Gray whales

Eschrichtius robustus. See Gray whales

Eyelids of lizards, R 2: 251
Eyes, moving flatfish, F 358

F

Face flies, I 2: 340
Fairy armadillos. See Pink fairy armadillos
Fairy bluebirds, B 4: 955–961
Fairy shrimps, CM 75–86
Fairy-wrens, Australian, B 4: 1070–1078
Falco peregrinus. See Peregrine falcons
Falco rusticolis. See Gyrfalcons
Falconets, B 1: 207, 229
Falconidae. See Caracaras; Falcons
Falconiformes. See Diurnal birds of prey
Falconry, B 1: 209, 230
Falcons, B 1: 207, 208–210, 229–239, B 2: 318
Falkland Island wolves, M 3: 581
False blind snakes, R 2: 309–313, 312 (ill.), 313 (ill.), 320
False coral snakes, R 2: 320, 326–330, 328 (ill.), 329 (ill.)
False gharials, R 1: 101–107, 108–109, 123–131
False pigs. See Pacaranas
False sunbirds, B 4: 801–806
False vampire bats, M 2: 323–329
False water cobras, R 2: 401
Family (Taxonomy), B 4: 861, F 257, M 1: 173
See also specific family names
Fan-tailed berrypeckers, B 5: 1199–1201, 1199 (ill.), 1200 (ill.)
Fannia species. See Little-house flies

Fantailed cisticolas. *See* Zitting cisticolas
Fantailed warblers. *See* Zitting cisticolas
Fantails, B 4: 1105–1114, B 5: 1354
Farming and wild animals, M 1: 72
Fasciola hepatica, CJ 95–96, 95 (ill.), 96 (ill.)
Fat innkeeper worms, CM 51
Fat-tailed dwarf lemurs, M 3: 445
Feather-footed jerboas. *See* Hairy-footed jerboas
Feather stars, CJ 181–187, 206
Feather-tailed possums, M 1: 102, 172–177
Feathers, grooming, B 1: 126
See also specific species
Feeding behavior, CJ 113
See also specific species
Felidae. See Cats
Feline owlet-nightjars, B 3: 594–595, 594 (ill.), 595 (ill.)
Felou gundis, M 5: 1083
Fennec foxes, M 3: 583
Ferret badgers, Chinese, M 3: 629
Ferrets, M 3: 581, 614, 615
Ferruginous pygmy-owls, B 3: 555
Fertilizer and salps, CJ 258
Ficedula basilanica. See Little slaty flycatchers
Fiddler crabs, sand, CM 133–134, 133 (ill.), 134 (ill.)
Fieldfares, B 4: 1015
Fiery minivets, B 4: 936, 940–941, 940 (ill.), 941 (ill.)
Figbirds, B 5: 1337–1344
Fighting fishes, Siamese, F 351–352, 351 (ill.), 352 (ill.)
Fiji Island boas, R 2: 343, 344
File snakes, R 2: 375–379

Filter-feeding whales. *See* Baleen whales
Filters, water, CM 101
Fin-footed mammals. *See* Marine carnivores
Fin whales, M 4: 796, 797
Finches, B 4: 789, B 5: 1278–1287, 1288
cardueline, B 5: 1289
cuckoo, B 5: 1308
Darwin's, R 1: 88
Gouldian, B 5: 1298
grassfinches, B 5: 1296–1305
Hawaiian, B 5: 1288
Laysan, B 5: 1293–1294, 1293 (ill.), 1294 (ill.)
New World, B 5: 1244–1257
snow, B 5: 1323–1324, 1323 (ill.), 1324 (ill.)
See also Weavers
Finding Nemo, F 230
Fingerprints, whale, M 4: 797
Finless dolphins, black, M 4: 715
Finless porpoises, M 4: 730
Fire ants, I 2: 394–395
Fire-bellied toads, A 1: 25–43, 30 (ill.), 31 (ill.)
Fire brats, I 1: 65–70
Fire-breasted flowerpeckers, B 5: 1197–1198, 1197 (ill.), 1198 (ill.)
Fire corals, CJ 45–46, 45 (ill.)
Fire-eyes, fringe-backed, B 4: 838
Fire gobies, F 320–321, 320 (ill.), 321 (ill.)
Fire salamanders, A 3: 443
Fire worms, CM 5–6, 5 (ill.), 6 (ill.)
Fireflies, I 2: 289, 294, 295
Fish and Wildlife Service (U.S.), B 2: 243
on Afro-American river turtles, R 1: 83

Flathead mullets, *F* 196–197, 196 (ill.), 197 (ill.)

Flatheads, F 247–255

Flattened musk turtles, *R 1:* 66

Fleas, *M 5:* 999, 1000, 1004

Fleas, I 2: 327–335

    lucerne, *I 1:* 53–54, 53 (ill.), 54 (ill.)

    snow, *I 1:* 52

    water, CM 75–86

Fleay's barred frogs, *A 1:* 128

Fleischmann's glass frogs, *A 2:* 243, 244, 246–248

Flesh flies, *I 2:* 336, 340

Fletcher's frogs, *A 1:* 124

Flies, I 2: 336–357

    alderflies, I 2: 262–267

    caddisflies, I 1: 94, I 2: 358–365

    common names for, *I 2:* 361

    damselflies, I 1: 81–91

    dobsonflies, I 2: 262–267

    dragonflies, I 1: 81–91

    fireflies, *I 2:* 289, 294, 295

    fishflies, I 2: 262–267

    hangingflies, I 2: 320–326

    mayflies, I 1: 71–80, 94

    owlflies, *I 2:* 273, 274, 275

    salmonflies, *I 1:* 96–97, 96 (ill.), 97 (ill.)

    sawflies, I 2: 390–414

    scorpionflies, I 2: 320–326

    snakeflies, I 2: 268–272

    spongilla, *I 2:* 274, 275

    stoneflies, I 1: 92–98

    whiteflies, *I 2:* 236, 237, 241–242, 241 (ill.), 242 (ill.)

Flightless birds, *B 2:* 318, 358, *B 3:* 518

Floating spotted frogs. *See* Pointed-tongue floating frogs

Flood, Bob, *B 1:* 62

Floodplain toadlets, *A 1:* 141

Florida gars, *F* 38

Florida lancelets, *CJ* 273–274, 273 (ill.), 274 (ill.)

Florida manatees. *See* West Indian manatees

Florida panthers, *M 3:* 658, 667

Florida wormlizards, R 1: 191, **203–207**, 205 (ill.), 206 (ill.)

Flounders, peacock, *F* 359–360, 359 (ill.), 360 (ill.)

Flowerpeckers, B 5: 1194–1201

Flowerpot blind snakes, *R 2:* 303

Flufftails, *B 2:* 356, 360–361, 360 (ill.), 361 (ill.)

Flukes, CJ 88–96

Fluvous leaf-nosed bats, *M 2:* 340

Fly River turtles. *See* Pig-nose turtles

Flycatchers, *B 4:* 789

    monarch, *B 5:* 1115–1122

    Old World, B 4: 1060–1069

    silky, B 4: 979–987

    tyrant, B 4: 850–859, 861, 872, 882

    See also Fantails; Gray hypocolius; Great kiskadees; Jacky winters

Flying foxes, *M 2:* 283, 284

    gigantic, *M 2:* 282

    Indian, *M 2:* 288–289, 288 (ill.), 289 (ill.)

    Malayan, *M 2:* 275–276

    See also Marianas fruit bats

Flying frogs, *A 3:* 350, 352

Flying gurnards, *F* 247

Flying jewels. *See* Hummingbirds

Flying lemurs. *See* Colugos

Flying lizards, *R 1:* 146, 153–154, 153 (ill.), 154 (ill.)

Flying snakes, *R 2:* 400

Flying squirrels, *M 5:* 998, 1008, 1009–1010, 1011–1012, 1011 (ill.), 1012 (ill.)

Flyingfishes, *F* 202–203, 205–206, 205 (ill.), 206 (ill.)

Foam nest frogs. *See* Gray treefrogs

Fodies, *B 5:* 1306

Follicle mites. *See* Hair follicle mites

Folohy golden frogs. *See* Arboreal mantellas

Food, scatterhoarding, *M 1:* 125

Food web and extinction, *R 2:* 229

Foreign species, *M 1:* 65

Forest bright-eyed frogs, *A 3:* 351, 354

Forest elephants, *M 4:* 816, 817–819, 817 (ill.), 818 (ill.)

Forest giants, *I 1:* 84, 88–90, 88 (ill.), 89 (ill.)

Forest green treefrogs. *See* Kinugasa flying frogs

Forest hogs, *M 4:* 895–896, 895 (ill.), 896 (ill.)

Forest monkeys, *M 3:* 425

Forests, sclerophyll, *B 4:* 1095

Forficula auricularia. See European earwigs

Fork-crowned lemurs, *M 3:* 444, 445

Forktailed drongos, *B 5:* 1346

The Formation of Vegetable Mould through the Action of Worms with Observations on Their Habits (Darwin), *CM* 19

Formicariidae. See Ant thrushes

Forty-spotted pardalotes, *B 5:* 1204

Fossa, M 3: 637–648, 644 (ill.), 645 (ill.)

Fossil frogs, *A 1:* 10

Galagidae. *See* Bushbabies

Galago senegalensis. See Senegal bushbabies

Galápagos cormorants, *B 1:* 116

Galápagos doves, *B 3:* 509

Galápagos fur seals, *M 3:* 674

Galápagos penguins, *B 1:* 71, 73

Galápagos sea lions, *M 3:* 674, 680–682, 680 (ill.), 681 (ill.)

Galápagos tortoises, *R 1:* 88, 90–91, 90 (ill.), 91 (ill.)

Galathea, *CM* 248

Galaxiids, F 121–126

Galbula pastazae. See Coppery-chested jacamars

Galbula ruficauda. See Rufous-tailed jacamars

Galbulidae. *See* Jacamars

Galeocerdo cuvier. See Tiger sharks

Galeodes arabs. See Camel spiders

Galidia elegans. See Ring-tailed mongooses

Galidinae, *M 3:* 637

Gall gnats, *I 2:* 341

Gallagher's free-tailed bats, *M 2:* 402

Gallicolumba luzonica. See Luzon bleeding hearts

Galliformes. *See* Chicken-like birds

Gallinago nigripennis. See African snipes

Gallinules, *B 2:* 316, 356, 357–358, 401

Galliwasps, R 2: 260–266

Gambian rats, *M 5:* 1066–1068, 1066 (ill.), 1067 (ill.)

Ganges dolphins, M 4: 709–713, 711 (ill.), 712 (ill.)

Gannets, B 1: 99–100, 125–133

Garden symphylans, *I 2:* 435, 436–437, 436 (ill.)

Gardiner's frogs, **A** *1:* 117–118, 119–120

Garnett's bushbabies. *See* Northern greater bushbabies

Garnett's galagos. *See* Northern greater bushbabies

Gars, F 37–40

Garter snakes
   common, *R 2:* 400, 405–406, 405 (ill.), 406 (ill.)
   Eastern, *R 1:* 141
   San Francisco, *R 2:* 406

Gasteropelecus sternicla. See River hatchetfishes

Gasterosteiformes, F 233–241

Gasterosteus aculeatus. See Threespine sticklebacks

Gastric brooding frogs, **A** *1:* 141, 142

Gastrophryne carolinensis. See Eastern narrow-mouthed toads

Gastropoda. *See* Limpets; Sea slugs; Snails

Gastrotrica. *See* Gastrotrichs

Gastrotrichs, CJ 123–127

Gavia immer. See Common loons

Gavia stellata. See Red-throated loons

Gavialidae. *See* Gharials

Gavialis gangeticus. See Gharials

Gavials. *See* Gharials

Gaviidae. *See* Loons

Gaviiformes. *See* Loons

Gazella thomsonii. See Thomson's gazelles

Gazelles, Thomson's, *M 4:* 978–980, 978 (ill.), 979 (ill.)

Geckos, R 1: 177–185

Geese, B 2: 241–245, 246–260

Gekkonidae. *See* Geckos; Pygopods

Genera, *B 4:* 861
   See also specific genera

Genets, M 3: 580, 582, **628–636**

Genetta genetta. See Common genets

Gentle lemurs, *M 3:* 426

Genus (Taxonomy), *F* 257, *R 2:* 321

Geochelone nigra. See Galápagos tortoises

Geococcyx californiana. See Greater roadrunners

Geoducks, *CM* 275

Geoemydidae. *See* Eurasian pond and river turtles; Neotropical wood turtles

Geoffroy's spider monkeys, *M 3:* 531–532, 531 (ill.), 532 (ill.)

Geography cone shells, *CM* 272–273, 272 (ill.), 273 (ill.)

Geomyidae. *See* Pocket gophers

Gerhardt, Gary, *M 4:* 964

German cockroaches, *I 1:* 100, 106–107, 106 (ill.), 107 (ill.), 113

German shepherds, *M 3:* 581

Gerrhonotus liocephalus. See Texas alligator lizards

Gervais's funnel-eared bats, *M 2:* 379

Gerygones, *B 4:* 1079, 1080, 1081

Ghana cuckoo-shrikes, *B 4:* 937

Gharas, *R 1:* 109

Gharials, R 1: 101–107, 108–113, 111 (ill.), 112 (ill.)
   See also False gharials

Ghost bats, M 2: 304–311
   See also Australian false vampire bats

Ghost-faced bats, *M 2:* 358

Ghost frogs, A 1: 110–116

Ghost moths, *I 2:* 367

Ghost owls. *See* Barn owls

Giant Amazonian leeches, *CM* 30–31, 30 (ill.), 31 (ill.)

Glossina palpalis. See Tsetse flies

Glossophaga soricina. See Pallas's long-tongued bats

Glossy-mantled manucodes, B 5: 1389

Glyptodonts, M 1: 178

Gnatcatchers, blue-gray, B 4: 1051, 1055–1057, 1055 (ill.), 1056 (ill.)

Gnathophausia ingens. See Giant red mysids

Gnathophausia species, CM 147

Gnathostomulida. See Gnathostomulids

Gnathostomulids, CJ 163–166

Gnats, I 2: 341

Gnu. See Black wildebeest

Go-away-birds, gray, B 3: 539, 542–543, 542 (ill.), 543 (ill.)

Goannas, R 2: 279–287

Goat fleas. See Sheep and goat fleas

Goats, M 4: 890, 969–987

Goatsuckers. See Nightjars

Gobies, F 317–325

Gobiesocoidei. See Clingfishes; Singleslits

Gobioidei. See Gobies

Godwits, B 2: 454

Goeldi's monkeys, M 3: 425, 496–508, 502 (ill.), 503 (ill.)

Gold in termite mounds, I 1: 121

Gold-striped frogs, A 2: 153–154, 173–175, 173 (ill.), 174 (ill.)

Golden bats. See Old World sucker-footed bats

Golden-bellied tree shrews, M 2: 265

Golden-breasted whistlers. See Golden whistlers

Golden-cheeked gibbons, M 3: 552

Golden-cheeked warblers, B 5: 1260

Golden coquis, A 2: 156

Golden-crowned kinglets, B 4: 1051

Golden-crowned sifakas, M 3: 459

Golden dart-poison frogs, A 2: 218, 226–228, 226 (ill.), 227 (ill.)

Golden doves, B 3: 504

Golden-headed lion tamarins, M 3: 498

Golden langurs, M 3: 423

Golden lion tamarins, M 3: 423, 498

Golden mantellas, A 3: 353–355

Golden moles, M 2: 213, 216, 226–231

Golden perches, F 265–266, 265 (ill.), 266 (ill.)

Golden plovers, B 2: 446

Golden poison frogs. See Golden dart-poison frogs

Golden ringtails, M 1: 156

Golden-rumped sengis, M 5: 1223, 1224, 1225

Golden spectacled lizards, R 2: 228

Golden-striped salamanders, A 3: 457–458, 457 (ill.), 458 (ill.)

Golden swallows, B 4: 915

Golden toads, A 2: 199, 203, 214–216, 214 (ill.), 215 (ill.)

Golden treefrogs, A 3: 352

Golden whistlers, B 5: 1133–1135, 1133 (ill.), 1134 (ill.)

Golden-winged sunbirds, B 5: 1215–1216, 1215 (ill.), 1216 (ill.)

Goldfinches, American, B 5: 1282–1284, 1282 (ill.), 1283 (ill.)

Goldfishes, F 85

Goldie's birds of paradise, B 5: 1390

Golfball frogs. See Northern spadefoot toads

Goliath frogs, A 1: 1, A 2: 288, 296–298, 296 (ill.), 297 (ill.)

Goliath herons, B 1: 144

Gomeran giant lizards, R 2: 223

Gondwana, M 1: 26

Gongylus gongylodes. See Wandering violin mantids

Gonoleks, B 4: 962, 963

Gonorynchiformes, F 79–83

Gooey-ducks. See Geoducks

Gooneys. See Laysan albatrosses

Gooseneck barnacles, CM 196

Gooseneck turtles. See Spiny softshells

Gophers, pocket, M 5: 997, 998, 999, 1029–1035

Gopherus agassizii. See Desert tortoises

Gordian knot and Alexander the Great, CJ 144

Gordian worms. See Hair worms

Gorilla gorilla. See Western gorillas

Gorillas, M 3: 423, 424, 563–564, 568–570, 568 (ill.), 569 (ill.)

Gouldian finches, B 5: 1298

Gould's frogmouths, B 3: 587

Grackles, B 5: 1268, 1269

Grainy Cochran frogs, A 2: 243

Grallina cyanoleuca. See Australian magpie-larks

Grallinidae. See Mudnest builders

Grampas. See Giant whip scorpions

Granite night lizards, R 2: 215

Grant's desert golden moles, M 2: 226, 229–231, 229 (ill.), 230 (ill.)

Grass cutters. See Cane rats

Grass frogs. See Brown frogs

Grass grubs, I 2: 372

Grass lizards, R 2: 222, 243, 244, 245

Greater bulldog bats, *M 2:* 364, 365, 367–369, 367 (ill.), 368 (ill.)

Greater bushbabies, *M 3:* 436, 441–442, 441 (ill.), 442 (ill.)

Greater cane rats, *M 5:* 1097–1098, 1100–1101, 1100 (ill.), 1101 (ill.)

Greater dog-faced bats, *M 2:* 309–310, 309 (ill.), 310 (ill.)

Greater dog-like bats. *See* Greater dog-faced bats

Greater five-lined skinks. *See* Broad-headed skinks

Greater flamingos, *B 1:* 203–205, 203 (ill.), 204 (ill.)

Greater gliders, *M 1:* 157–158, 157 (ill.), 158 (ill.)

Greater gliding possums, *M 1:* 154–160

Greater hoopoe-larks, *B 4:* 908–909, 908 (ill.), 909 (ill.)

Greater horseshoe bats, *M 2:* 331, 333–335, 333 (ill.), 334 (ill.)

Greater leaf-folding frogs, *A 3:* 332, 333, 334

Greater marsupial moles. *See* Southern marsupial moles

Greater melampittas, *B 4:* 1100

Greater New Zealand short-tailed bats, *M 2:* 372, 373

Greater painted snipes, *B 2:* 407, 408–409, 410–412, 410 (ill.), 411 (ill.)

Greater racket-tailed drongos, *B 5:* 1350–1351, 1350 (ill.), 1351 (ill.)

Greater rhabdornis, *B 5:* 1188, 1190

Greater rheas, *B 1:* 13

Greater roadrunners, *B 3:* 545, 549–550, 549 (ill.), 550 (ill.)

Greater sac-winged bats, *M 2:* 307–308, 307 (ill.), 308 (ill.)

Greater scythebills, *B 4:* 832

Greater thornbirds, *B 4:* 827–829, 827 (ill.), 828 (ill.)

Grebes, *B 1:* 90–97

Green anacondas, *R 1:* 140, *R 2:* 342, 343–344, 350–351, 350 (ill.), 351 (ill.)

Green and black poison frogs, *A 2:* 220, 221–223, 222

Green anoles, *R 1:* 174–175, 174 (ill.), 175 (ill.)

Green bonellias, *CM* 53–54, 53 (ill.), 54 (ill.)

Green burrowing frogs, *A 3:* 390, 392, 393

Green crabs, European, *CM* 125

Green frogs, *A 2:* 289–290, 303

Green ioras, *B 4:* 957

Green lacewings, *I 2:* 274–275, 276, 277, 278–279, 278 (ill.), 279 (ill.)

Green magpies, *B 5:* 1398, 1405–1406, 1405 (ill.), 1406 (ill.)

Green morays, *F* 64–65, 64 (ill.), 65 (ill.)

Green peafowl, *B 2:* 266

Green poison frogs. *See* Green and black poison frogs

Green puddle frogs. *See* Pointed-tongue floating frogs

Green pythons, *R 2:* 358–359, 358 (ill.), 359 (ill.)

Green rain frogs. *See* Madagascar rain frogs

Green ringtails, *M 1:* 154

Green seaturtles, *R 1:* 25, 26, 27–29, 27 (ill.), 28 (ill.)

Green swordtails, *F* 214–215, 214 (ill.), 215 (ill.)

Green toads, *A 2:* 199

Green tree monitors, *R 2:* 280

Green tree pythons. *See* Green pythons

Green treefrogs, *A 2:* 281–283, 281 (ill.), 282 (ill.)

Green woodhoopoes, *B 3:* 710–712, 710 (ill.), 711 (ill.)

Greenbuls, *B 4:* 944, 945–946

Greenhouse camel crickets, *I 1:* 177–178, 177 (ill.), 178 (ill.)

Greenhouse whiteflies, *I 2:* 241–242, 241 (ill.), 242 (ill.)

Greenlings, *F* 247–249

Grenadier weavers. *See* Southern red bishops

Grenadiers, *F* 173–180

Grevy's zebras, *M 4:* 857–859, 857 (ill.), 858 (ill.)

Grieving elephants, *M 4:* 811

Griffon vultures, *B 1:* 207

Grindles. *See* Bowfins

Grinnells. *See* Bowfins

Grooming, mutual, *M 3:* 517

Grooming feathers, *B 1:* 126

Grosbeak weavers, *B 5:* 1306

Ground antbirds, *B 4:* 836

Ground beetles, *I 2:* 290, 293, 295, 296, 297–298

Ground boas, Calabar, *R 2:* 344

Ground cuckoo-shrikes, *B 4:* 935, 936

Ground cuscuses, *M 1:* 119–120, 119 (ill.), 120 (ill.)

Ground-hornbills
    Abyssinian, *B 3:* 653–654
    southern, *B 3:* 717–719, 717 (ill.), 718 (ill.)

Ground jays, Hume's, *B 5:* 1398

Ground pangolins, *M 5:* 993–995, 993 (ill.), 994 (ill.)

Ground pythons. *See* Neotropical sunbeam snakes

Ground-rollers, *B 3:* 691, 692, 693

Ground sloths, lesser Haitian, *M 1:* 183

Ground squirrels, *M 5:* 998, 1008, 1009, 1010

Groupers, Nassau, *F* 269–270, 269 (ill.), 270 (ill.)

Grouse, *B 2:* 298

Harlequin toads. *See* Harlequin frogs

Harp seals, *M 3:* 692–694, 692 (ill.), 693 (ill.)

Harpactes oreskios. See Orange-breasted trogons

Harris's hawks, *B 1:* 213, 217–218, 217 (ill.), 218 (ill.)

Harvestman, common, *I 1:* 15, 27–28, 27 (ill.), 28 (ill.)

Hatchetfishes, river, *F* 98–99, 98 (ill.), 99 (ill.)

Hatching, asynchronous, *B 2:* 476

> *See also* specific species

Hawaiian acorn worms, *CJ* 244–245, 244 (ill.), 245 (ill.)

Hawaiian creepers, *B 5:* 1288

Hawaiian crows, *B 5:* 1400

Hawaiian finches, *B 5:* 1288

Hawaiian honeycreepers, *B 5:* 1209, **1288–1295**

Hawaiian monk seals, *M 3:* 582, 691, 698–700, 698 (ill.), 699 (ill.)

Hawk moths, *I 2:* 369, 387–388, 387 (ill.), 388 (ill.)

Hawks, *B 1:* 207, 208, 209, **212–222,** 230

Hawksbill seaturtles, *R 1:* 26

Hay's Spring amphipods, *CM* 186

Head lice, *I 2:* 230, 231–233, 231 (ill.), 232 (ill.)

Heart-nosed bats, *M 2:* 280, 323

Heart-winged bats, *M 2:* 325

Heartworms, canine, *CJ* 138, 139–140, 139 (ill.)

Hector's dolphins, *M 4:* 737–738, 740

Hedge sparrows, *B 4:* **991–996**

Hedgehog tenrecs, *M 2:* 233–234

Hedgehogs, *M 2:* 213, 215, 216, **218–224**

Heel-walkers, *I 1:* **188–192,** 191 (ill.), 192 (ill.)

Hees. *See* Pacas

Heleophryne natalensis. See Natal ghost frogs

Heleophrynidae. *See* Ghost frogs

Heliornis fulica. See Sungrebes

Heliornithidae. *See* Sungrebes

Helix pomatia. See Roman snails

Hellbenders, *A 3:* **419–426,** 423 (ill.), 424 (ill.)

Helmet shrikes, *B 4:* 962, 964

Helmet vangas, *B 4:* 972, 973, 975

Helmeted guineafowl, *B 2:* 291–292, 291 (ill.), 292 (ill.)

Helmeted hornbills, *B 3:* 720–721, 720 (ill.), 721 (ill.)

Helmeted turtles, *R 1:* 73–75, 73 (ill.), 74 (ill.)

Helmeted water toads, *A 2:* 153, 155

Helminthophis flavoterminatus, *R 2:* 290

Helminthophis species, *R 2:* 240

Heloderma suspectum. See Gila monsters

Helodermatidae. *See* Gila monsters; Mexican beaded lizards

Hemicentetes semispinosus. See Yellow-streaked tenrecs

Hemichordata. *See* Hemichordates

Hemichordates, *CJ* **241–247**

Hemidactylus frenatus. See House geckos

Hemingway, Ernest, *F* 335

Hemiphractus proboscideus. See Sumaco horned treefrogs

Hemiprocne coronata. See Crested tree swifts

Hemiprocnidae. *See* Tree swifts

Hemiptera, *I 2:* **236–256**

Hemisotidae. *See* Shovel-nosed frogs

Hemisquilla ensigera, CM 95

Hemisus barotseensis, *A 2:* 326

Hemisus marmatorus, *A 2:* 327

Hemisus sudanensis. See Marbled snout-burrowers

Hemithyris psittacea. See Black lampshells

Hercules beetles, *I 2:* 290, 306–307, 306 (ill.), 307 (ill.)

Hermits, hairy, *B 3:* 632–633, 632 (ill.), 633 (ill.)

Herons, *B 1:* 143, 144, 145, 146, **149–159,** 186

Herpestidae. *See* Fossa; Mongooses

Herpestinae, *M 3:* 637

Herrings, *F* 73–78

Heterocephalus glaber. See Naked mole-rats

Heterodon platirhinos. See Eastern hog-nosed snakes

Heteromyidae. *See* Kangaroo mice; Kangaroo rats; Pocket mice

Heteropteryx dilatata. See Jungle nymphs

Hewitt's ghost frogs, *A 1:* 113

Hexaprotodon liberiensis. See Pygmy hippopotamuses

Hibernation and turtles, *R 1:* 65

Hicketies. *See* Central American river turtles

Hickman's pygmy mountain shrimps, *CM* 106

Hidden-neck turtles, *R 1:* 9, 14, 77, 78

Hide beetles, *I 2:* 290, 293

Hierro giant lizards, *R 2:* 224

Highland tinamous, *B 1:* 8–10, 8 (ill.), 9 (ill.)

Highland tuco-tucos, *M 5:* 1167, 1168

Hildebrandt's horseshoe bats, *M 2:* 330

Himalaya flying frogs, *A 3:* 352

Himalayan accentors, *B 4:* 992

Himalayan vultures, *B 1:* 212

Horsfield's bronze-cuckoos, *B 4*: 1071, 1089

Hose's palm civets, *M 3*: 630

Host species, *CJ* 149, *CM* 238, *I 2*: 229, 328–329
   See also specific species

Hourglass treefrogs, **A** *2*: 271–273, 271 (ill.), 272 (ill.)

House centipedes, *I 2*: 421–423, 421 (ill.), 422 (ill.)

House flies, *I 2*: 336, 337, 340

House geckos, *R 1*: 183–184, 183 (ill.), 184 (ill.)

House sparrows, *B 5*: 1319, 1320–1322, 1320 (ill.), 1321 (ill.)

House wrens, *B 4*: 1038, 1039, 1043–1044, 1043 (ill.), 1044 (ill.)

Houston toads, **A** *2*: 199, 201–202, 204

Hover flies, *I 2*: 336, 339

Howler monkeys, *M 3*: 425, **526–535**

Hubbard's angel insects, *I 2*: 219–220, 219 (ill.), 220 (ill.)

Hubei fire-bellied toads. *See* Small-webbed bell toads

Huias, *B 5*: 1354–1355

Hula painted frogs, **A** *1*: 45, 48

Human blood flukes, *CJ* 90, 93–94, 93 (ill.), 94 (ill.)

Human fleas, *I 2*: 328, 330

Human head/body lice, *I 2*: 231–233, 231 (ill.), 232 (ill.)

Humans, *M 3*: 423, **563–577**, 574 (ill.), 575 (ill.)

Hume's ground jays, *B 5*: 1398

Hummingbirds, *B 3*: 610–614, **630–638**, 669, *B 5*: 1208

Humpback whales, *M 4*: 797, 802–803, 802 (ill.), 803 (ill.)

Hurricanes, *B 1*: 104

Huso huso. See Beluga sturgeons

Hutchinsoniella macracantha, *CM* 73–74, 73 (ill.), 74 (ill.)

Hutias, *M 5*: **1188–1193**

Hyacinth macaws, *B 3*: 522

Hyaenidae. *See* Aardwolves; Hyenas

Hyalinobatrachium crybetes, **A** *2*: 248

Hyalinobatrachium valerioi. See La Palma glass frogs

Hydra (Mythology), *CJ* 43

Hydrobatidae. *See* Storm-petrels

Hydrochaeridae. *See* Capybaras

Hydrochaeris hydrochaeris. See Capybaras

Hydrocynus goliath. See Giant tigerfishes

Hydrodamalis gigas. See Steller's sea cows

Hydroids, *CJ* **42–52**

Hydrolagus colliei. See Spotted ratfishes

Hydrophasianus chirurgus. See Pheasant-tailed jacanas

Hydrophiidae, *R 2*: 415

Hydrothermal vent worms, *CM* **39–44**, 42 (ill.), 43 (ill.)

Hydrozoa. *See* Hydroids

Hyenas, *M 3*: 578, 580, **649–656**

Hyla leucophyllata. See Hourglass treefrogs

Hylidae. *See* Amero-Australian treefrogs

Hylobates lar. See Lar gibbons

Hylobates pileatus. See Pileated gibbons

Hylobatidae. *See* Gibbons

Hylochoerus meinertzhageni. See Forest hogs

Hymenocera picta. See Harlequin shrimps

Hymenochirus species. *See* Dwarf clawed frogs

Hymenoptera. *See* Ants; Bees; Sawflies; Wasps

Hymenopus coronatus. See Orchid mantids

Hynobiidae. *See* Asiatic salamanders

Hynobius retardatus. See Hokkaido salamanders

Hyperoliidae. *See* African treefrogs

Hyperolius viridiflavus. See Painted reed frogs

Hyperoodon ampullatus. See Northern bottlenosed whales

Hypocolius, gray, *B 4*: 979, 980, 985–986, 985 (ill.), 986 (ill.)

Hypocolius ampelinus. See Gray hypocolius

Hypophthalmichthys molitrix. See Silver carps

Hypothymis azurea. See Black-naped monarchs

Hypsipetes madagascariensis. See Black bulbuls

Hypsiprymnodon moschatus. See Musky rat-kangaroos

Hypsiprymnodontidae. *See* Musky rat-kangaroos

Hyracoidea. *See* Hyraxes

Hyraxes, *M 4*: **820–827**

Hystricidae. *See* Old World porcupines

Hystricidae species, *M 5*: 1112

Hystricopsylla schefferi, *M 5*: 1004

Hystrix africaeaustralis. See South African porcupines

Hystrix indica. See Indian crested porcupines

Hystrix species, *M 5*: 1111–1112

I

Iberian green frogs, **A** *1*: 49

Iberian lynx, *M 3*: 581, 658

Iberian midwife toads, **A** *1*: 44, 46–47

Iberian painted frogs, **A** *1*: 47

Iberian parsley frogs, **A** *1*: 102–103, 104

Iberian water frogs. *See* Iberian green frogs

Jackson's chameleons, *R 1:* 157, 159 (ill.), 160–161, 160 (ill.)

Jacky winters, *B 5:* 1125–1126, 1125 (ill.), 1126 (ill.)

Jade treefrogs, *A 3:* 352

Jaegers, *B 2:* 475–477

Jamaica giant galliwasps, *R 2:* 262–263

Jamaican hutias. *See* Brown's hutias

Jamaican todies, *B 3:* 669, *B 4:* 988

Jambato toads, *A 2:* 203

James's flamingos, *B 1:* 202

Japanese beetles, *I 2:* 293

Japanese clawed salamanders, **A** 3: 411, 415–416, 415 (ill.), 416 (ill.)

Japanese cranes. *See* Red-crowned cranes

Japanese fire-bellied newts, **A** 3: 455–456, 455 (ill.), 456 (ill.)

Japanese giant salamanders, **A** 3: 419–420, 422

Japanese macaques, *M 3:* 423

Japanese sea lions, *M 3:* 581

Japanese spider crabs, *CM* 121

Japanese treefrogs. *See* Kinugasa flying frogs

Japanese waxwings, *B 4:* 979

Japanese white-eyes, *B 5:* 1222–1223, 1222 (ill.), 1223 (ill.)

Jaragua lizards, *R 1:* 140

Java file snakes, *R 2:* 376, 377

Java frogs. *See* Pointed-tongue floating frogs

Java sparrows, *B 5:* 1298

Javan leaf insects, *I 1:* 208–209, 208 (ill.), 209 (ill.)

Javan pigs, *M 4:* 894

Javan plovers, *B 2:* 446

Javan rhinoceroses, *M 4:* 875, 876

Javan slit-faced bats, *M 2:* 318

Javanese lapwings, *B 2:* 446

Javelinas. *See* Collared peccaries

Jaw animals, CJ 160–162

Jaws of snakes, *R 2:* 344

Jays, *B 4:* 789, *B 5:* 1398–1410

Jefferson, Thomas, *B 4:* 998

Jellyfish, CJ 52–66, F 344
    See also Comb jellies

Jerboas, *M 5:* 997, 998, 1044–1050

Jerdon's palm civets, *M 3:* 630

Jerdon's pratincoles, *B 2:* 438

Jersey tiger moths, *I 2:* 370

Jersey Wildlife Preservation Trust, *R 2:* 365

Jesus birds. *See* Jacanas

Jesus lizards. *See* Brown basilisk lizards

Jewel-babblers, *B 4:* 1099, 1101

Jewel thrushes. *See* Pittas

Jewels of the forest. *See* Pittas

John dories, *F* 230

Johnstone's crocodiles, *R 1:* 123

Juan Fernández fur seals, *M 3:* 674

Jumping hares. *See* Springhares

Jumping mice, *M 5:* 1044–1050, 1062–1063, 1062 (ill.), 1063 (ill.)

Jumping spiders, zebra, *I 1:* 29–31, 29 (ill.), 30 (ill.)

Jungle nymphs, *I 1:* 197, 198–199, 198 (ill.), 199 (ill.)

Jurassic frogs. *See* Fossil frogs

Jurassic Park, R 1: 5

Jynx torquilla. See Northern wrynecks

K

Kagus, *B 2:* 316, 317–318, 349–355, 353 (ill.), 354 (ill.)

Kakarratuls. *See* Southern marsupial moles

Kalahari sand lizards, *R 2:* 222

Kalinowski's tinamous, *B 1:* 7

Kaloula pulchra. See Malaysian painted frogs

Kangaroo emus, *B 1:* 27

Kangaroo Island dunnarts, *M 1:* 58

Kangaroo mice, *M 5:* 1036–1043

Kangaroo rats, *M 5:* 997, 998, 1036–1043

Kangaroos, *M 1:* 26, 99–104, 130, 135–148
    See also Rat-kangaroos

Karora, *M 1:* 81

Kartana, I. Nyoman, *M 4:* 928

Kassina senegalensis. See Bubbling kassinas

Kassinas, *A 3:* 335
    See also Bubbling kassinas; Yellow-legged kassinas

Katydids, *I 1:* 166–187

Keel-billed motmots, *B 3:* 678

Keel-scaled splitjaw snakes, *R 2:* 363–367

Kemp's longbills, *B 4:* 1052

Kemp's ridley seaturtles, *R 1:* 26

Kerala caecilians, *A 3:* 517–521

Kerodon rupestris. See Rock cavies

Kestrels, *B 1:* 208, 229

Keyhole limpets, *CM* 261

Kiangs, *M 4:* 860–861, 860 (ill.), 861 (ill.)

Killdeer, *B 2:* 447–449, 447 (ill.), 448 (ill.)

Killer box jellies. *See* Box jellies

Killer whales, *M 4:* 706, 737, 738, 741–743, 741 (ill.), 742 (ill.), 780

Killifishes, *F* 210–218

King birds of paradise, *B 5:* 1395–1397, 1395 (ill.), 1396 (ill.)

King cobras, *R 2:* 421–444, 421 (ill.), 422 (ill.)

Laniidae. *See* Shrikes

Lanius ludovicianus. See Loggerhead shrikes

Lanternfishes, F 148–152

Lanza's alpine salamanders, **A** *3:* 443

Lapas. *See* Pacas

Lapwings, B *2:* **444–452**

Lar gibbons, **M** *3:* 556–558, 556 (ill.), 557 (ill.)

Large blues, **I** *2:* 376–377, 376 (ill.), 377 (ill.)

Large-eared tenrecs, **M** *2:* 233

Large-footed tree shrews, **M** *2:* 265

Large frogmouths, **B** *3:* 587

Large golden moles, **M** *2:* 227

Large-spined bell toads, **A** *1:* 29

Largemouth basses, **F** 261–262, 261 (ill.), 262 (ill.)

Largescale foureyes, **F** 212–213, 212 (ill.), 213 (ill.)

Laridae, B *2:* **475–485**

Larks, B *4:* **901–912, B** *5:* 1360, 1361, 1362–1364, 1362 (ill.), 1363 (ill.)

Larus saundersi. See Saunder's gulls

Larvaceans, CJ 263–266

Larvae, nauplius, *CM* 198

Las Vegas leopard frogs, **A** *2:* 291–292

Laterallus jamaicensis. See Black rails

Laticauda colubrina. See Sea kraits

Latimeria chalumnae. See Coelacanths

Latrine flies, **I** *2:* 340

Laughing hyenas. *See* Spotted hyenas

Laughing kookaburras, **B** *3:* 655, 660, 661–663, 661 (ill.), 662 (ill.)

Laughing thrushes, **B** *4:* 1026

Laurasia, **M** *1:* 26

Laysan albatrosses, **B** *1:* 45, 50–52, 50 (ill.), 51 (ill.)

Laysan finches, **B** *5:* 1293–1294, 1293 (ill.), 1294 (ill.)

Lazy toads, **A** *1:* 77

Leadbeater's possums, **M** *1:* 163

Leaf cutter ants, **I** *2:* 392, 396, 400–402, 400 (ill.), 401 (ill.)

Leaf-folding frogs, **A** *3:* 335

Leaf insects, I *1:* **193–210**

Leaf litter frogs, **A** *1:* 77, 79

Leaf-loves, **B** *4:* 950–951, 950 (ill.), 951 (ill.)

Leaf miner flies, **I** *2:* 341

Leaf-miner moths, **I** *2:* 366, 372

Leaf monkeys, **M** *3:* 424, 536, 537

Leaf-nosed bats
   American, M *2:* **345–357**
   Old World, M *2:* **339–344**

Leaf-rollers, **I** *2:* 372

Leafbirds, B *4:* **955–961**

Leafhoppers, corn, **I** *2:* 318, 319

Leafy seadragons, **F** 237–238, 237 (ill.), 238 (ill.)

Least shrews, American, **M** *2:* 250–251, 250 (ill.), 251 (ill.)

Least weasels, **M** *3:* 578, 614

Leatherback seaturtles, R *1:* 10, 24, **44–49,** 47 (ill.), 48 (ill.)

Leatherback turtles. *See* Spiny softshells

Leeches, CM 25–32

Legless lizards, **R** *2:* 260, 262
   See also Blindskinks

Legless skinks, **R** *2:* 250

Leiopelma hamiltoni. See Hamilton's frogs

Leiopelma pakeka. See Maud Island frogs

Leiopelmatidae. *See* New Zealand frogs

Leiothrix, Astley's, **B** *4:* 1027

Leipoa ocellata. See Malleefowl

Lemmings, **B** *2:* 455, **M** *5:* 996, 1051, 1056–1057, 1056 (ill.), 1057 (ill.)

Lemmus lemmus. See Norway lemmings

Lemur catta. See Ringtailed lemurs

Lemur coronatus. See Crowned lemurs

Lemuridae. *See* Lemurs

Lemuroid ringtail possums, **M** *1:* 156

Lemurs, M *3:* 423, 424, 426, **450–457**
   baboon, **M** *3:* 459
   black, **M** *3:* 424
   dwarf, M *3:* **444–449**
   mouse, M *3:* 423, **444–449**
   sloth, **M** *3:* 459
   sportive, M *3:* **466–471**
   woolly, **M** *3:* 459
   See also Colugos

Leodia sexiesperforata. See Six keyhole sand dollars

Leopard frogs, **A** *2:* 287, 289–290

Leopard moths, giant, **I** *2:* 370

Leopards, snow, **M** *3:* 668–669, 668 (ill.), 669 (ill.)

Lepeophtheirus salmonis. See Salmon lice

Lepidobatrachus laevis. See Budgett's frogs

Lepidodermella squamata, CJ 125–126, 125 (ill.), 126 (ill.)

Lepidoptera. *See* Butterflies; Moths; Skippers

Lepidosiren paradoxa. See South American lungfishes

Lepidurus packardi, CM 80

Lepilemur leucopus. See White-footed sportive lemurs

Lepilemur ruficaudatus. See Red-tailed sportive lemurs

Liposcelis bostrychophilia. See Book lice

Lipotes vexillifer. See Baijis

Lipotidae. *See* Baijis

Lithodytes lineatus. See Gold-striped frogs

Litoria caerulea. See Green treefrogs

Little brown bats, *M 2:* 417–418, 417 (ill.), 418 (ill.)

Little file snakes, *R 2:* 375, 376, 377, 378–379, 378 (ill.), 379 (ill.)

Little-house flies, *I 2:* 340

Little slaty flycatchers, *B 4:* 1065–1066, 1065 (ill.), 1066 (ill.)

Little spotted kiwis, *B 1:* 30

Live-bearers, F 210–218

Livestock, domestic, *M 4:* 890

Living fossils, *I 1:* 9, *R 2:* 274

Lizardfishes, F 142–147

Lizards, *R 1:* 2, 132, **139–144**
  alligator, *R 2:* **260–266**
  blue spiny, *R 1:* 169
  brown basilisk, *R 1:* 168
  Chinese crocodile, *R 2:* 268, 269
  dragon, *R 1:* 140, **145–155**
  earless monitor, *R 2:* **279–287**
  eyelids of, *R 2:* 251
  girdled, *R 2:* **243–248**
  horned, *R 1:* 167, 169
  knob-scaled, *R 2:* **267–272,** 271 (ill.), 272 (ill.)
  Mexican beaded, *R 1:* 143, *R 2:* **273–278**
  microteiid, *R 2:* **228–234**
  monitor, *R 1:* 140, 141, *R 2:* **279–287**
  night, *R 2:* **215–220**
  plated, *R 2:* **243–248**
  rock, *R 2:* **221–227**
  short-horned, *R 1:* 169
  tails of, *R 2:* 223, 244

wall, *R 2:* **221–227**

whiptail, *R 1:* 142, *R 2:* **235–242**
  zebra-tailed, *R 1:* 168
  See also Monitors; Pygopods; Wormlizards

Llamas, *M 4:* **916–926,** 924 (ill.), 925 (ill.)

Loaches, *F* 84–85, 90–91, 90 (ill.), 91 (ill.)

Lobsters, CM 121–137

Locusts, *I 1:* 169, 171

Loggerhead shrikes, *B 4:* 962, 963, 968–970, 968 (ill.), 969 (ill.)

Loggerhead turtles, *R 1:* 26, 30–31, 30 (ill.), 31 (ill.)

Logrunners, B 4: 1093–1098

Loligo pealeii. See Longfin inshore squids

Lonchura punctulata. See Spotted munias

Long-armed chafers, *I 2:* 291

Long-beaked echidnas, *M 1:* 2, 3, 5, 7, 8, 10

Long-billed curlews, *B 2:* 459–460, 459 (ill.), 460 (ill.)

Long-bodied cellar spiders, *I 1:* 32–33, 32 (ill.), 33 (ill.)

Long-eared bats, *M 2:* 278
  See also Lesser New Zealand short-tailed bats

Long-eared owls, *B 3:* 565

Long-faced potoroos, *M 1:* 132

Long-fingered slender toads, *A 2:* 205–207, 205 (ill.), 206 (ill.)

Long-fingered stream toads. *See* Long-fingered slender toads

Long-haired spider monkeys, *M 3:* 425

Long-nosed echidnas. *See* Long-beaked echidnas; Rufous spiny bandicoots

Long-snouted dolphins. *See* Spinner dolphins

Long-spined sea urchins, *CJ* 214, 215–216, 215 (ill.), 216 (ill.)

Long-tailed bats. *See* Hardwicke's lesser mouse-tailed bats; Mouse-tailed bats

Long-tailed chinchillas, *M 5:* 1131, 1132–1134, 1132 (ill.), 1133 (ill.)

Long-tailed fantails, *B 4:* 1109

Long-tailed manakins, *B 4:* 867–868, 867 (ill.), 868 (ill.)

Long-tailed paradigallas, *B 5:* 1390

Long-tailed pygmy possums, *M 1:* 150

Long-tailed seps, Eastwood's, *R 2:* 245

Long-tailed shrews, *M 2:* 214, 247

Long-tailed titmice, B 5: 1151–1157

Long-toed treefrogs, *A 3:* 337–338

Long-tongued bats, Pallas's, *M 2:* 353–354, 353 (ill.), 354 (ill.)

Long-winged coneheads, *I 1:* 181–182, 181 (ill.), 182 (ill.)

Longbills, Kemp's, *B 4:* 1052

Longclaws, *B 4:* 924–927, 930–931, 930 (ill.), 931 (ill.)

Longdong stream salamanders, *A 3:* 410

Longfin inshore squids, *CM* 297–298, 297 (ill.), 298 (ill.)

Longhorns, *I 2:* 290, 294, 295

Longnose lancetfishes, *F* 144–145, 144 (ill.), 145 (ill.)

Longnose stub-foot toads, *A 2:* 203

Longtail tadpole shrimps, *CM* 79, 81–83, 83 (ill.), 84 (ill.)

Loons, B 1: 82–89

Lophelia pertusa. See Deep water reef corals

Lophiiformes. *See* Anglerfishes

Magdalena river turtles, *R 1:* 72

Magdelena tinamous, *B 1:* 7

Magellan diving-petrels, *B 1:* 67

Magellanic penguins, *B 1:* 79–80, 79 (ill.), 80 (ill.)

Magellanic plovers, *B 2:* 445, 446

Magellanic tuco-tucos, *M 5:* 1168

Maggots, *I 2:* 337, 340

Magicicada septendecim. See Seventeen-year cicadas

Magnificent frigatebirds, *B 1:* 112–114, 112 (ill.), 113 (ill.)

Magpie geese, *B 2:* 242

Magpie-larks, Australian, *B 5:* 1360–1364, 1362 (ill.), 1363 (ill.)

Magpie-robins, *B 4:* 1016

Magpie-shrikes, *B 5:* **1372–1379**

Magpies, *B 5:* 1398, 1400
   Australian, *B 5:* 1372–1374
   green, *B 5:* 1398, 1405–1406, 1405 (ill.), 1406 (ill.)

Mahogany gliders, *M 1:* 163

Majungatholus atopus, R 1: 3

Makaira nigricans. See Blue marlins

Ma'kech beetles, *I 2:* 297

Malabar civets, *M 3:* 581, 629

Malacosteus niger. See Rat-trap fishes

Malagasy civets, *M 3:* 630

Malagasy mongooses, *M 3:* 637

Malagasy ring-tailed mongooses, *M 3:* 641, 642

Malagasy variable reed frogs, *A 3:* 332

Malaita fantails, *B 4:* 1109

Malay mouse deer, lesser, *M 4:* 928, 930–932, 930 (ill.), 931 (ill.)

Malayan colugos, *M 2:* 269, 270, 272–274, 272 (ill.), 273 (ill.)

Malayan flying foxes, *M 2:* 275–276

Malayan flying lemurs. *See* Malayan colugos

Malayan gharials. *See* False gharials

Malayan moonrats, *M 2:* 218, 223–224, 223 (ill.), 224 (ill.)

Malayan porcupines, *M 5:* 1114

Malayan tapirs, *M 4:* 871–873, 871 (ill.), 872 (ill.)

Malaysian honeyguides, *B 3:* 768, 769–770, 769 (ill.), 770 (ill.)

Malaysian painted frogs, *A 3:* 369, 374, 381–383, 381 (ill.), 382 (ill.)

Malaysian plovers, *B 2:* 446

Malaysian sun bears, *M 3:* 593, 594

Malcolm's Ethiopian toads, *A 2:* 202

Maleos, *B 2:* 276–277, 276 (ill.), 277 (ill.)

Malimbes, *B 5:* 1306

Mallada albofascialis. See Green lacewings

Mallards, *B 2:* 247, 254–255, 254 (ill.), 255 (ill.)

Malleefowl, *B 2:* 270, 273–275, 273 (ill.), 274 (ill.)

Mallorcan midwife toads, *A 1:* 45, 46–48, 49

Maluridae. *See* Australian fairy-wrens

Malurus splendens. See Splendid fairy-wrens

Mambas, *R 2:* 416

Mamos, *B 5:* 1288

Manakins, *B 4:* **864–871**

Manatees, *M 4:* **828–832, 841–847**

Manaus slender-legged treefrogs, *A 2:* 262–263

Mandarin salamanders, **A** *3:* 453–455, 453 (ill.), 454 (ill.)

Mandrills, *M 3:* 423–425, 536, 548–549, 548 (ill.), 549 (ill.)

Mandrillus sphinx. See Mandrills

Maned sloths, *M 1:* 191

Maned wolves, *M 3:* 590–591, 590 (ill.), 591 (ill.)

Mangabeys, *M 3:* 424, 425

Mangrove fantails, *B 4:* 1106

Manidae. *See* Pangolins

Manis temminckii. See Ground pangolins

Manta birostris. See Atlantic mantas

Mantas, Atlantic, *F* 17–18, 17 (ill.), 18 (ill.)

Mantellas, *A 3:* 351, 352–353

Mantidactylus liber. See Free Madagascar frogs

Mantidflies, *I 2:* 273, 274, 275–276

Mantids, *I 1:* 99, **135–151,** 189

Mantis religiosa. See European mantids

Mantis shrimps, CM 92–99

Mantodea. *See* Mantids

Mantophasmatodea. *See* Gladiators; Heel-walkers

Manucodes, glossy-mantled, *B 5:* 1389

Manus fantails, *B 4:* 1109

Manx shearwaters, *B 1:* 54, 56–57, 56 (ill.), 57 (ill.)

Marabou storks, *B 1:* 166

Maras, *M 5:* 999, **1139–1146,** 1144 (ill.), 1145 (ill.)

Marble sleepers, *F* 324–325, 324 (ill.), 325 (ill.)

Marbled caecilians, *A 3:* 508–509, 508 (ill.), 509 (ill.)

Marbled murrelets, *B 2:* 488

Marbled shovel-nosed frogs. *See* Marbled snout-burrowers

Marbled snout-burrowers, *A 2:* 323–324, 325, 327 (ill.)

Megascolides australis. See Gippsland giant worms

Megophryidae. *See* Asian toadfrogs

Megophrys montana. See Asian horned frogs

Meiacanthus grammistes. See Striped poison-fang blennies

Melampittas, *B 4:* 1099, 1100

Melanocharis versteri. See Fan-tailed berrypeckers

Melanogrammus aeglefinus. See Haddocks

Melbourne Water Department, *M 1:* 22

Meleagris gallopavo. See Wild turkeys

Meles meles. See European badgers

Melichneutes robustus. See Lyre-tailed honeyguides

Meliphagidae. *See* Australian honeyeaters

Melitta species, *I 2:* 394

Melodious larks, *B 4:* 903, 905

Melospiza melodia. See Song sparrows

Melville, Herman, *M 4:* 761, 788

Menhadens, *F* 73

Mentawai macaques, *M 3:* 537

Menura alberti. See Albert's lyrebirds

Menuridae. *See* Lyrebirds

Mephitis mephitis. See Striped skunks

Merlins, *B 1:* 229

Mermis nigrescens, CJ 135–136, 136 (ill.)

Meropidae. *See* Bee-eaters

Meropogon forsteni. See Purple-bearded bee-eaters

Merops apiaster. See European bee-eaters

Merostomata. *See* Horseshoe crabs

Merten's water monitors, *R 2:* 280

Mesites, *B 2:* 316, 317, **320–325**

Mesitornis variegata. See White-breasted mesites

Mesitornithidae. *See* Mesites; Roatelos

Mesoamerican burrowing toads, *A 1:* **56–61,** 59 (ill.), 60 (ill.)

Mesoamerican river turtles. *See* Central American river turtles

Mesonerilla prospera, CM 3–4

Mespilia globulus. See Tuxedo pincushion urchins

Metridium senile. See Frilled anemones

Mexican beaded lizards, *R 1:* 143, *R 2:* **273–278**

Mexican burrowing pythons. *See* Neotropical sunbeam snakes

Mexican burrowing toads. *See* Mesoamerican burrowing toads

Mexican caecilians, *A 3:* 530–532, 530 (ill.), 531 (ill.)

Mexican dippers. *See* American dippers

Mexican free-tailed bats. *See* Brazilian free-tailed bats

Mexican funnel-eared bats, *M 2:* 378, 380–381, 380 (ill.), 381 (ill.)

Mexican giant musk turtles, *R 1:* 64, 66

Mice, *M 5:* 996–1000, **1051–1068**
    birch, *M 5:* 1044–1050
    jumping, *M 5:* 1044–1050, 1062–1063, 1062 (ill.), 1063 (ill.)
    kangaroo, *M 5:* 1036–1043
    marsupial, *M 1:* 56–63
    pocket, *M 5:* 998, 1036–1043
    See also Dormice

Michoacan pocket gophers, *M 5:* 1032

Micrixalus phyllophilus. See Nilgiri tropical frogs

Micro frogs, *A 2:* 293–295, 293 (ill.), 294 (ill.)

Microbatrachella capensis. See Micro frogs

Microbiotheria. *See* Monitos del monte

Microbiotheriidae. *See* Monitos del monte

Microbiotherium species, *M 1:* 44

Microcebus rufus. See Red mouse lemurs

Microchiroptera, *M 2:* 275, 276–278, 282, 323, 339

Microcoryphia. *See* Bristletails

Microeca fascinans. See Jacky winters

Micrognathozoa. *See* Jaw animals

Microhylidae. *See* Narrow-mouthed frogs

Micropsyche ariana, I 2: 366

Micropteropus pusillus. See Dwarf epauletted fruit bats

Micropterus salmoides. See Largemouth basses

Microraptor species, *R 1:* 3

Microteiids, *R 2:* **228–234**

Micrurus fulvius. See North American coral snakes

Mictacea. *See* Mictaceans

Mictaceans, CM 160–164

Mictocaris halope, CM 161, 162–163, 162 (ill.), 163 (ill.)

Midges, *I 2:* **336–357**

Midgut, neuroptera, *I 2:* 276

Midwife toads, *A 1:* **44–55,** 50 (ill.), 51 (ill.)

Migrant shrikes. *See* Loggerhead shrikes

Migration
    bats, *M 2:* 411
    birds, *B 1:* 54, 145, *B 3:* 613
    seaturtles, *R 1:* 25
    See also specific species

Milk, crop, *B 3:* 506, 509
Milkfishes, F 79–83, 81 (ill.), 82 (ill.)
Milksnakes, *R 2:* 401, 407–408, 407 (ill.), 408 (ill.)
Milky storks, *B 1:* 166
Millepora alcicornis. See Fire corals
Millipedes, *I 2:* **425–433**
Milne-Edwards's sifakas, *M 3:* 460–461, 460 (ill.), 461 (ill.)
Mimetica mortuifolia. See Dead leaf mimeticas
Mimeticas, dead leaf, *I 1:* 183–184, 183 (ill.), 184 (ill.)
Mimicry, *A 2:* 219–220, *R 2:* 415
    See also Defense mechanisms; specific species
Mimidae. *See* Mockingbirds; Thrashers
Minahass masked owls, *B 3:* 559
Minas Gerais tyrannulets, *B 4:* 853
Mindanao tree shrews, *M 2:* 265
Miniopterus schreibersi. See Common bentwing bats
Minivets, fiery, *B 4:* 936, 940–941, 940 (ill.), 941 (ill.)
Minke whales
    Antarctic, *M 4:* 786
    northern, *M 4:* 800–801, 800 (ill.), 801 (ill.)
Minks, *M 3:* 581, 615
Minnows, F 84–91
    See also Mudminnows
Miracle triplefins, *F 303–304,* 303 (ill.), 304 (ill.)
Mirafra javanica. See Australasian larks
Mirapinna esau. See Hairyfishes
Mirounga angustirostris. See Northern elephant seals
Missing link, arthropod to annelida, *CM 57*

Mississippi cranes, *B 2:* 340
Mississippi gopher frogs. *See* Dusky gopher frogs
Mistletoebirds, *B 5:* 1195
Mistletoes, *M 1:* 44
Mitchell's plovers, *B 2:* 445, 446
Mites, *I 1:* **15–44**
Mniotilta varia. See Black-and-white warblers
Moby Dick (Melville), *M 4:* 761, 788
Mocha Island degus, *M 5:* 1173
Mockingbirds, *B 4:* **997–1003**
Mocquard's rain frogs, *A 3:* 390–391, 393, 395–397, 395 (ill.), 396 (ill.)
Moho bishopi. See Bishop's oos
Mohua ochrocephala. See Yellowheads
Moisture and surface-to-volume ratio, *R 2:* 297
Mole crickets, *I 1:* 168, 170–171
Mole-limbed wormlizards, *R 1:* 191, **197–202,** 204
Mole-rats, African, *M 5:* 998, **1103–1110**
Mole salamanders, *A 3:* **433–439**
Mole skinks, bluetail, *R 2:* 252
Mole vipers. *See* African burrowing snakes
Moles, *M 2:* 214, 216, **255–262,** *M 5:* 998
    golden, *M 2:* 213, 216, **226–231**
    marsupial, *M 1:* **94–98**
    shrew, *M 2:* **255–262**
Moloch gibbons, *M 3:* 552
Molossidae. *See* Free-tailed bats; Mastiff bats
Moluccan woodcocks, *B 2:* 456
Momotidae. *See* Motmots
Momotus momota. See Blue-crowned motmots

Mona boas, *R 2:* 345
Mona Island blind snakes, *R 2:* 305
Monachus schauinslandi. See Hawaiian monk seals
Monarch butterflies, *I 2:* 370
Monarch flycatchers, *B 5:* **1115–1122**
Monarchidae. *See* Monarch flycatchers
Money, shell, *CM 290*
Mongolian larks, *B 4:* 903
Mongooses, *M 3:* 578, 580, 582, **637–648**
Moniliformis moniliformis, CJ 150–151, 150 (ill.), 151 (ill.)
Monitors, *R 1:* 141, *R 2:* **279–287**
    See also Earless monitors
Monitos del monte, *M 1:* **44–50,** 46 (ill.), 47 (ill.)
Monk seals
    Caribbean, *M 3:* 581, 691
    Hawaiian, *M 3:* 582, 691, 698–700, 698 (ill.), 699 (ill.)
    Mediterranean, *M 3:* 581, 691
Monk sloths, *M 1:* 189, 190
Monkey-faced owls. *See* Common barn owls
Monkeys, *M 1:* 170, *M 3:* 423–426
    capuchin, *M 3:* 426, **487–495**
    Goeldi's, *M 3:* 425, **496–508,** 502 (ill.), 503 (ill.)
    howler, *M 3:* 425, **526–535**
    night, *M 3:* 425, **509–515**
    Old World, *M 3:* 423, 424, **536–550**
    sea, *CM 78*
    spider, *M 3:* 425, **526–535**
    squirrel, *M 3:* 424, **487–495**

Monkfishes, *F* 191–192, 191 (ill.), 192 (ill.)

Monoblastozoa. *See* Salinella

Monodon monoceros. See Narwhals

Monodontidae. *See* Belugas; Narwhals

Monogamy, *B* 2: 327, 367
    See also specific species

Monogeneans, CJ 97–102

Monoplacophora. *See* Monoplacoporans

Monoplacoporans, CM 247–251

Monotremata. *See* Monotremes

Monotremes, *M* 1: 1–6

Monstrilla grandis, CM 226–227, 226 (ill.), 227 (ill.)

Montane alligator lizards, *R* 2: 262

Montifringilla nivalis. See Snow finches

Mooneyes, *F* 47

Moonrats, *M* 2: 213, 218, 219, 223–224, 223 (ill.), 224 (ill.)

Moorhens, *B* 2: 356–365

Moorish idols, *F* 332–333, 332 (ill.), 333 (ill.)

Moose, *M* 4: 948–950, 948 (ill.), 949 (ill.)

Morays, F 60–67

Morelets treefrogs, *A* 2: 264

Morelia viridis. See Green pythons

Mormon crickets, *I* 1: 169, 171

Mormoopidae. *See* Moustached bats

Moroccan glass lizards, *R* 2: 260, 261

Morpho menelaus. See Blue morphos

Morris, John, *M* 4: 928

Morris, Kathy, *M* 4: 928

Morus bassanus. See Northern gannets

Moschus moschiferus. See Siberian musk deer

Mosquitoes, *I* 2: 336–357

Moss animals. *See* Ectoprocts

Moss bugs, *I* 2: 236

Moss frogs, *A* 1: 141–142

Motacilla cinerea. See Gray wagtails

Motacillidae. *See* Pipits; Wagtails

Moth flies, sugarfoot, *I* 2: 341

Moth lacewings, *I* 2: 273, 274, 276, 280–281, 280 (ill.), 281 (ill.)

Moths, *I* 2: 366–389, *M* 1: 151

Motmots, *B* 3: 653, 654, 655–656, 676–681

Mottled burrowing frogs. *See* Marbled snout-burrowers

Mottled shovel-nosed frogs. *See* Marbled snout-burrowers

Mottled tuco-tucos, *M* 5: 1168

Motyxia species, *I* 2: 427

Moundbuilders, *B* 2: 270–278

Mount Glorious day frogs, *A* 1: 143

Mount Glorious torrent frogs. *See* Mount Glorious day frogs

Mountain alligators. *See* Hellbenders

Mountain beavers, *M* 5: 1003–1007, 1005 (ill.), 1006 (ill.)

Mountain cows. *See* Tapirs

Mountain frogs, *A* 1: 128

Mountain hares, *M* 5: 1218–1219, 1218 (ill.), 1219 (ill.)

Mountain lions. *See* Pumas

Mountain owlet-nightjars, *B* 3: 592

Mountain pacas, *M* 5: 1160–1161, 1162

Mountain plovers, *B* 2: 446

Mountain pygmy possums, *M* 1: 101, 102, 149, 150, 151

Mountain short-legged toads. *See* Slender mud frogs

Mountain tapirs, *M* 4: 848, 849, 865

Mountain-toucans, gray-breasted, *B* 3: 759, 761–762, 761 (ill.), 762 (ill.)

Mountain viscachas, *M* 5: 1129, 1130

Mountain yellow-legged frogs, *A* 2: 292

Mountain zebras, *M* 4: 849

Mourning cloaks, *I* 2: 371

Mourning doves, American, *B* 3: 513–514, 513 (ill.), 514 (ill.)

Mouse bandicoots, *M* 1: 88, 89

Mouse deer, *M* 4: 887, 928, 930–932, 930 (ill.), 931 (ill.)

Mouse Deer and Crocodile (Morris and Kartana), *M* 4: 928

Mouse lemurs, *M* 3: 423, 444–449

Mouse opossums. *See* Shrew opossums

Mouse-tailed bats, *M* 2: 298–303

Mousebirds, *B* 3: 639–643

Moustache shrimps. *See* Mystacocarids

Moustache toads, *A* 1: 77

Moustached bats, *M* 2: 358–363

Moustached monkeys, *M* 3: 425

Moustached tree swifts, *B* 3: 624

Moustached woodcreepers, *B* 4: 832

Mud devils. *See* Hellbenders

Mud-divers. *See* Parsley frogs

Mud turtles
    African, *R* 1: 70
    American, *R* 1: 10, 64–69
    Broadley's, *R* 1: 72
    Seychelles, *R* 1: 72

Mudfishes, African, *F* 79, 80
    See also Bowfins

Mudminnows, F 116–120

Mudnest builders, *B* 5: 1360–1365

Names
origin, *CJ* 23, 43, 117, 144, 173, 206
scientific, *F* 257, *R 2:* 321
See also specific species

Nannophrys guentheri, **A** 2: 291–292

Nannosquilla decemspinosa, CM 96–97, 96 (ill.), 97 (ill.)

Narceus americanus, I 2: 427–428

Narrow-billed todies, *B 3:* 669, 672

Narrow-headed frogs. *See* Web-foot frogs

Narrow-mouthed frogs, A *3:* **368–389**

Narwhals, *M 4:* 767–776, 773 (ill.), 774 (ill.)

Nasalis larvatus. See Proboscis monkeys

Nasikabatrachidae. *See Nasikabatrachus sahyadrensis*

Nasikabatrachus sahyadrensis, **A** *1:* 118, 119

Nassau groupers, *F* 269–270, 269 (ill.), 270 (ill.)

Nasutitermes nigriceps. See Black-headed nasute termites

Natal ghost frogs, **A** *1:* 110–111, 112, 114–116, 114 (ill.), 115 (ill.)

Natalidae. *See* Funnel-eared bats

Natalus species, *M 2:* 379

Natalus stramineus. See Mexican funnel-eared bats

Natterer's tuco-tucos, *M 5:* 1168

Nauplius larvae, *CM* 198

Nautilids, CM 293–305

Nautilus pompilius. See Pearly nautiluses

Navassa woodsnakes, *R 2:* 371

Nebalia bipes, CM 88

Nectarinia, B 5: 1208–1209

Nectariniidae. *See* Sunbirds

Necturus maculosus. See Mudpuppies

Needle beaks. *See* Rufous-tailed jacamars

Needlefishes, F 202–209

Nemaster rubiginosa. See Orange sea lilies

Nemateleotris magnifica. See Fire gobies

Nematodes, *CJ* 133

Nemertea. *See* Anoplans; Enoplans

Nemoptera sinuata. See Spoonwing lacewings

Neobalaenidae. *See* Pygmy right whales

Neobatrachus pictus. See Painted frogs

Neocyamus physeteris. See Sperm whale lice

Neodrepanis coruscans. See Common sunbird-asities

Neophron percnopterus. See Egyptian vultures

Neopilina galathea, CM 248

Neotropical sunbeam snakes, *R 2:* **337–341,** 339 (ill.), 340 (ill.)

Neotropical wood turtles, *R 1:* **58–63,** 77

Nesomimus macdonaldi. See Hood mockingbirds

Nests
burrow, *B 2:* 414
snakeskin, *B 5:* 1390
See also specific species

Net-winged beetles, *I 2:* 289

Neuroptera, I 2: 273–288

New Caledonian crows, *B 5:* 1399

New Caledonian owlet-nightjars, *B 3:* 593

New Guinea bush frogs, **A** *3:* 368–369, 370

New Guinea forest rails, *B 2:* 356

New Guinea logrunners, *B 4:* 1093, 1094, 1095

New Guinea snake-necked turtles, *R 1:* 19

New Mexico spadefoot toads, **A** *1:* 97

New South Wales National Park, *B 4:* 1077

New South Wales Threatened Species Conservation Act, *M* 2: 297

New World anteaters, *M 1:* 9

New World blackbirds, *B 5:* **1268–1277**

New World finches, *B 5:* **1244–1257**

New World leaf-nosed bats. *See* American leaf-nosed bats

New World marsupials, *M 1:* 26

New World monkeys, *M 3:* 423

New World opossums, *M 1:* **24–36**

New World pond turtles, *R 1:* **50–57,** 77

New World porcupines, *M 5:* **1121–1128**

New World pythons. *See* Neotropical sunbeam snakes

New World quails, *B 2:* **303–309**

New World sucker-footed bats. *See* Disk-winged bats

New World toucans, *B 3:* 654

New World vultures, *B 1:* **143–148, 175–185,** 187

New World warblers, *B 5:* **1258–1267**

New Zealand dotterels, *B 2:* 446

New Zealand frogs, A *1:* **8–16,** 18

New Zealand long-eared bats. *See* Lesser New Zealand short-tailed bats

New Zealand Red Data Book, *M 2:* 376

New Zealand short-tailed bats, *M 2:* **371–377**

Northern muriquis, *M 3:* 527

Northern Pacific albatrosses, *B 1:* 45

Northern Pacific right whales, *M 4:* 789

Northern Pacific sea stars, *CJ* 196–197, 196 (ill.), 197 (ill.)

Northern pikas, *M 5:* 1210–1211, 1210 (ill.), 1211 (ill.)

Northern raccoons, *M 3:* 605, 606, 607–609, 607 (ill.), 608 (ill.)

Northern ravens, *B 5:* 1398, 1409–1410, 1409 (ill.), 1410 (ill.)

Northern ribbon snakes, *R 2:* 401

Northern rock-crawlers, *I 1:* 153, 155–156, 155 (ill.), 156 (ill.)

Northern saw-whet owls, *B 3:* 565

Northern screamers, *B 2:* 262

Northern sea lions, *M 3:* 582

Northern short-tailed bats. *See* Lesser New Zealand short-tailed bats

Northern snake-necked turtles, *R 1:* 20

Northern spadefoot toads, *A 1:* 135–137, 135 (ill.), 136 (ill.)

Northern stargazers, *F* 296–297, 296 (ill.), 297 (ill.)

Northern tamanduas, *M 1:* 179, 195

Northern three-toed jerboas. *See* Hairy-footed jerboas

Northern toadlets, *A 1:* 139

Northern tuataras, *R 1:* 132–135, 136–137, 136 (ill.), 137 (ill.)

Northern wrynecks, *B 3:* 777–778, 777 (ill.), 778 (ill.)

Norway lemmings, *M 5:* 1056–1057, 1056 (ill.), 1057 (ill.)

Norwegian tubeworms, *CM* 36–37, 36 (ill.), 37 (ill.)

Nosy Mangabe Special Reserve, *M 3:* 476

Notaden melanoscaphus. See Northern spadefoot toads

Notharchus macrorhynchos. See White-necked puffbirds

Nothocercus bonapartei. See Highland tinamous

Notomys alexis. See Australian jumping mice

Notonecta sellata. See Backswimmers

Notoplana acticola, CJ 83–84, 83 (ill.), 84 (ill.)

Notoryctemorphia. See Marsupial moles

Notoryctes typhlops. See Southern marsupial moles

Notoryctidae. See Marsupial moles

Notothenioidei. See Southern cod-icefishes

Notothens, emerald, *F* 290–291, 290 (ill.), 291 (ill.)

Novodinia antillensis. See Velcro sea stars

Nsoung long-fingered frogs, *A 2:* 312, 314

Nucifraga caryocatactes. See Spotted nutcrackers

Nukupuus, *B 5:* 1288

Numbats, *M 1:* 9, 52, 53, **64–68,** 66 (ill.), 67 (ill.)

Numida meleagris. See Helmeted guineafowl

Numididae. See Guineafowl

Nunlets, rufous-capped, *B 3:* 744–745, 744 (ill.), 745 (ill.)

Nuptial pads, *A 1:* 20
  See also specific species

Nutcrackers, spotted, *B 5:* 1407–1408, 1407 (ill.), 1408 (ill.)

Nuthatches, *B 5:* **1173–1181,** 1179 (ill.), 1180 (ill.)

Nutrias. *See* Coypus

Nyctea scandiaca. See Snowy owls

Nycteridae. See Slit-faced bats

Nycteris thebaica. See Egyptian slit-faced bats

Nyctibiidae. See Potoos

Nyctibius griseus. See Gray potoos

Nycticebus pygmaeus. See Pygmy slow lorises

Nyctimene robinsoni. See Queensland tube-nosed bats

Nyctixalus pictus. See Painted Indonesian treefrogs

O

Oahu deceptor bush crickets, *I 1:* 171

Oarfishes, *F* 154, 155–156, 155 (ill.), 156 (ill.)

Oaxacan dwarf boas, *R 2:* 369

Oaxacon pocket gophers, *M 5:* 1032

O'Brien, Mark, *B 2:* 271

Occidozyga lima. See Pointed-tongue floating frogs

Ocean pouts, *F* 285–286, 285 (ill.), 286 (ill.)

Oceanites oceanicus. See Wilson's storm-petrels

Ochotona hyperborea. See Northern pikas

Ochotona hyperborean yesoensis, M 5: 1211

Ochotona princeps. See American pikas

Ochotonidae. See Pikas

Octodon degus. See Degus

Octodontidae. See Octodonts

Octodonts, *M 5:* **1172–1176**

Octopods, CM 293–305

Octopus vulgaris. See Common octopuses

Octopuses. *See* Octopods

Ocypus oiens. See Devil's coach-horses

Odd-toed ungulates, *M 4:* **848–853**

Oriolidae. *See* Figbirds; Old World orioles

Oriolus oriolus. See Eurasian golden orioles

Ornate narrow-mouthed frogs, A *3*: 368, 374

Ornate shrews, Buenea Vista Lake, M *2*: 216, 249

Ornithischia, R *1*: 1–2

Ornithomimids, R *1*: 4

Ornithoptera alexandrae. See Queen Alexandra's birdwings

Ornithoptera species. *See* Birdwing butterflies

Ornithorhynchidae. *See* Duck-billed platypus

Ornithorynchus anatinus. See Duck-billed platypus

Ortalis vetula. See Plain chachalacas

Orthonectida. *See* Orthonectidans

Orthonectidans, CJ 22–25

Orthonychidae. *See* Chowchillas; Logrunners

Orthonyx temminckii. See Southern logrunners

Orthoporus ornatus, I *2*: 426, 428

Orthoptera. *See* Crickets; Grasshoppers; Katydids

Orycteropodidae. *See* Aardvarks

Orycteropus afer. See Aardvarks

Osmeriformes, F 121–126

Osprey, B *1*: 215–216, 215 (ill.), 216 (ill.)

Osteoglossiformes, F 46–49

Ostracoda. *See* Mussel shrimps

Ostriches, B *1*: 1, 11, 35–40, 37 (ill.), 38 (ill.)

Otariidae. *See* Eared seals; Fur seals; Sea lions

Otididae. *See* Bustards

Otis tarda. See Great bustards

Otolemur garnettii. See Northern greater bushbabies

Otophryne pyburni. See Pyburn's pancake frogs

Otter civets, M *3*: 629

Otter shrews, M *2*: 232, 233, 234

Otters, M *3*: 579, 582, 614–627, 637, M *4*: 707

Otus asio. See Eastern screech-owls

Ouzels. *See* American dippers

Ovenbirds, B *4*: 821–829

Overfishing cod, F 175

Overseas Development Institute, M *4*: 889

Oviraptorids, R *1*: 5

Ovis canadensis. See Bighorn sheep

Owl monkeys. *See* Night monkeys

Owlet-frogmouths. *See* Owlet-nightjars

Owlet-nightjars, B *3*: 575, 576

Owlflies, I *2*: 273, 274, 275

Owls, B *3*: 552–556, 579, 585
   barn, B *3*: 557–563, 564, 565
   typical (Strigidae), B *3*: 557, 564–573

Owston's palm civets, M *3*: 630

Oxpeckers, red-billed, B *5*: 1334–1336, 1334 (ill.), 1335 (ill.)

Oxydactyla species, A *3*: 369

Oxyeleotris marmorata. See Marble sleepers

Oxyruncidae. *See* Sharpbills

Oxyruncus cristatus. See Sharpbills

Oyster leeches, CJ 85–86, 85 (ill.), 86 (ill.)

Oyster toadfishes, F 182, 184–185, 184 (ill.), 185 (ill.)

Oystercatchers, B *2*: 417–422

Oysters, CM 276, 277–278, 277 (ill.), 278 (ill.)

P

Pacaranas, M *5*: 1135–1138, 1137 (ill.), 1138 (ill.)

Pacas, M *5*: 1160–1165, 1163 (ill.), 1164 (ill.)

Pachycephala pectoralis. See Golden whistlers

Pachycephalidae. *See* Whistlers

Pachyramphus aglaiae. See Rose-throated becards

Pacific coast giant musk turtles, R *1*: 66

Pacific giant glass frogs, A *2*: 242–243, 244, 246–247, 255–258, 255 (ill.), 256 (ill.)

Pacific giant salamanders, A *3*: 427–432

Pacific golden plovers, B *2*: 396

Pacific halibuts, F 361–362, 361 (ill.), 362 (ill.)

Pacific monarchs. *See* Black-naped monarchs

Packman frogs. *See* Surinam horned frogs

Paddlefishes, F 32–36

Pads, nuptial, A *1*: 20
   See also specific species

Paghman mountain salamanders, A *3*: 410

Pagophilus groenlandicus. See Harp seals

Painted bullfrogs. *See* Malaysian painted frogs

Painted burrowing frogs. *See* Painted frogs

Painted buttonquails, B *2*: 331–332, 331 (ill.), 332 (ill.)

Painted frogs, A *1*: 44–55, 53 (ill.), 54 (ill.), 132–134, 132 (ill.), 133 (ill.)

Painted Indonesian treefrogs, A *3*: 354, 361–363, 362 (ill.)

Painted mantellas, A *3*: 351

Painted reed frogs, A *3*: 331, 336, 342–345, 342 (ill.), 343 (ill.)

Painted snipes, B *2*: 407–412

Painted terrapins, *R 1*: 60

Painted treefrogs, **A** *3*: 334

Painted turtles, *R 1*: 53–54, 53 (ill.), 54 (ill.), 77

Pakistani toads, **A** *1*: 2

Palawan tits, *B 5*: 1166

Palawan tree shrews, *M 2*: 265

Pale-billed sicklebills, *B 5*: 1390

Pale-browed tinamous, *B 1*: 7

Pale-faced sheathbills, *B 2*: 469

Pale throated sloths, *M 1*: 189

Paleothentidae, *M 1*: 39

Palla's mastiff bats, *M 2*: 276

Pallas's cormorants, *B 1*: 117

Pallas's long-tongued bats, *M 2*: 353–354, 353 (ill.), 354 (ill.)

Pallas's sandgrouse, *B 3*: 501–502, 501 (ill.), 502 (ill.)

Pallid bats, *M 2*: 413–414, 413 (ill.), 414 (ill.)

Pallid cuckoos, *B 4*: 1108

Pallid sturgeons, *F* 34

Palm civets, *M 3*: 579, 629, 630

Palm weevils, *I 2*: 298

Palmchats, *B 4*: **988–990**, 989 (ill.), 990 (ill.)

Palouse giant earthworms, *CM* 19

Pan troglodytes. See Chimpanzees

Panamanian dwarf boas, *R 2*: 370

Pandas
giant, *M 3*: 579, 593–595, 599–601, 599 (ill.), *600* (ill.)
red, *M 3*: 579–580, 605, 606, 610–612, 610 (ill.), 611 (ill.)

Pandinus imperator. See Emperor scorpions

Pandion haliaetus. See Osprey

Pangolins, *M 1*: 9, *M 5*: **989–995**

Panopea abrupta. See Geoducks

Panorpa nuptialis, I 2: 324–325, 324 (ill.), 325 (ill.)

Panorpa species, *I 2*: 322

Pantala flavescens. See Wandering gliders

Panthera leo. See Lions

Panthera tigris. See Tigers

Panthers, *M 3*: 658, 667
See also Pumas

Pantodon buchholzi. See Freshwater butterflyfishes

Paper wasps, *I 2*: 393, 395

Papuan pythons, *R 2*: 353

Papuan treecreepers, *B 5*: 1145

Papuan whipbirds, *B 4*: 1099

Parabuteo unicinctus. See Harris's hawks

Paradigallas, long-tailed, *B 5*: 1390

Paradiplogrammus bairdi. See Lancer dragonets

Paradisaeidae. *See* Birds of paradise

Paradise birds. *See* Birds of paradise

Paradise-flycatchers, African, *B 5*: 1117–1119, 1117 (ill.), 1118 (ill.)

Paradox frogs, *A 2*: 284–285, 284 (ill.), 285 (ill.)

Parafontaria laminata, I 2: 428

Paragordius varius, CJ 145–146, 145 (ill.), 146 (ill.)

Paraguayan caiman lizards, *R 2*: 236

Parakeet auklets, *B 2*: 486

Parakeets, *B 3*: 523, 524–525, 524 (ill.), 525 (ill.)

Paralithodes camtschaticus. See Red king crabs

Paranaspides lacustris. See Great lake shrimps

Parasites, *CJ* 18, 89
blood-sucking, *CM* 205
copepod, *CM* 222
twisted-wing, *I 2*: **315–319**, 318 (ill.), 319 (ill.)
See also specific species

Parasitic diseases, *CJ* 90
See also specific species

Parasitic earwigs, *I 1*: 159

Parasitic wasps, *I 2*: 392–393

Pardalotes, *B 5*: **1202–1207**

Pardalotidae. *See* Pardalotes

Pardalotus striatus. See Striated pardalotes

Parenting, cooperative, *M 3*: 497
See also specific species

Paridae. *See* Chickadees; Titmice

Parnell's moustached bats, *M 2*: 359, 361–363, 361 (ill.), 362 (ill.)

Parotias, Wahnes's, *B 5*: 1390

Parrotbills, *B 4*: 1025

Parrotfishes, *F* 272–274, 277–278, 277 (ill.), 278 (ill.)

Parrots, *B 3*: **522–537**

Parsley frogs, **A** *1*: **102–108**, 106 (ill.), 107 (ill.)

Parthenogenesis and lizards, *R 2*: 236

Partridges, *B 2*: 269

Parulidae. *See* New World warblers

Parus major. See Great tits

Passenger pigeons, *B 3*: 505, 510

Passer domesticus. See House sparrows

Passerculus sandwichensis. See Savanna sparrows

Passeridae. *See* Sparrows

Passeriformes. *See* Perching birds

Passerines. *See* Perching birds

Patagonia frogs, **A** *2*: 178–180, 178 (ill.), 179 (ill.)

Patagonian hares. *See* Maras

Patagonian maras. *See* Maras

Patagonian opossums, *M 1*: 25, 27–28

Paucituberculata. *See* Shrew opossums

Pauropoda. *See* Pauropods

Pauropods, I 2: 438–442

Paw Paw frogs, A 1: 128

Pawnee National Grasslands, M 4: 964

Pea aphids, I 2: 243–244, 243 (ill.), 244 (ill.)

Pea crabs, CM 121

Pea urchins, CJ 217–218, 217 (ill.), 218 (ill.)

Peacock flounders, F 359–360, 359 (ill.), 360 (ill.)

Peacock mantis shrimps, CM 95, 98–99, 98 (ill.), 99 (ill.)

Peafowl, green, B 2: 266

Peanut worms, CM 45–49

Pearl essence, F 74

Pearl mussels, CM 276

Pearl oysters, black-lipped, CM 277–278, 277 (ill.), 278 (ill.)

Pearlfishes, F 168, 170–172, 170 (ill.), 171 (ill.)

Pearls, CM 276

Pearly nautiluses, CM 299–300, 299 (ill.), 300 (ill.)

Pearly-skin puddle frogs. *See* Pointed-tongue floating frogs

Pearson's tuco-tucos, M 5: 1169–1170, 1169 (ill.), 1170 (ill.)

Peccaries, M 4: 902–906

Pedetidae. *See* Springhares

Peewees. *See* Australian magpie-larks

Pelagia noctiluca. See Nightlight jellyfish

Pelecanidae. *See* Pelicans

Pelecaniformes, B 1: 98–102

Pelecanoides urinatrix. See Common diving-petrels

Pelecanoididae. *See* Diving-petrels

Pelecanus erythrorhynchos. See American white pelicans

Pelecanus occidentalis. See Brown pelicans

Pelican Lagoon Research Center, M 1: 13

Pelicans, B 1: 98–102, 134–142, 186, M 2: 365

Pelobatidae. *See* Spadefoot toads

Pelodytes punctatus. See Parsley frogs

Pelodytidae. *See* Parsley frogs

Pelomedusa subrufa. See Helmeted turtles

Pelomedusidae. *See* African side-necked turtles

Peltopses, B 5: 1372–1374

Pen-tailed tree shrews, M 2: 263, 264

Penaeus monodon. See Giant tiger prawns

Penang Taylor's frogs, A 2: 290–291

Penduline titmice, B 5: 1158–1163

Penguins, B 1: 71–81, B 2: 470

Pennella balaenopterae, CM 220

Pentastomida. *See* Tongue worms

Peppershrikes, B 5: 1235–1243

Peprilus triacanthus. See Butterfishes

Pepsis grossa. See Tarantula hawks

Peramelemorphia, M 1: 74–78

Perameles gunnii. See Eastern barred bandicoots

Peramelidae. *See* Bandicoots; Bilbies

Perches, F 256–258, 259–271 climbing, F 349–350, 349 (ill.), 350 (ill.)

pirate, F 163, 164–165, 164 (ill.), 165 (ill.)

See also Surfperches; Troutperches

Perching birds, B 4: 789–792

Perciformes, F 256–258

Percoidei, F 259–271

Percopsiformes, F 162–166

Peregrine falcons, B 1: 209–210, 229, 236–238, 236 (ill.), 237 (ill.)

Perez's snouted frogs, A 2: 156, 167–169, 167 (ill.), 168 (ill.)

Pericrocotus igneus. See Fiery minivets

Periophthalmus barabarus. See Atlantic mudskippers

Periplaneta americana. See American cockroaches

Perissodactyla. *See* Odd-toed ungulates

Pernambuco pygmy owls, B 3: 565

Perodicticus potto. See Pottos

Perognathus inornatus. See San Joaquin pocket mice

Peropteryx kappleri. See Greater dog-faced bats

Peroryctidae. *See* Spiny bandicoots

Perret's snout-burrowers, A 2: 326

Peruvian diving-petrels, B 1: 67, 68

Peruvian plantcutters, B 4: 881–882, 883, 884–886, 884 (ill.), 885 (ill.)

Peruvian thick-knees, B 2: 433

Petalura ingentissima, I 1: 84

Petauridae. *See* Gliding possums; Striped possums

Petaurinae. *See* Gliding possums

Petauroides volans. See Greater gliders

Petaurus breviceps. See Sugar gliders

Peter's giant blind snakes, R 2: 302

Peter's treefrogs. *See* Painted Indonesian treefrogs

Petrels, B 1: 43, 53–60 diving-petrels, B 1: 67–70 storm-petrels, B 1: 41, 61–66

Piculets, *B 3:* 725, 774–788

Pied avocets, *B 2:* 424

Pied currawongs, *B 4:* 1108

Pied tamarins, *M 3:* 497

Pig-footed bandicoots, *M 1:* 77, 79, 82

Pig-nose turtles, *R 1:* **13–17**, 16 (ill.), 17 (ill.)

Pig-nosed frogs. *See* Marbled snout-burrowers

Pigeon lice, slender, *I 2:* 234–235, 234 (ill.), 235 (ill.)

Pigeons, *B 3:* 504–507, **508–516**, *I 2:* 235

Pigs, *M 4:* 890, **892–901**
    See also Aardvarks; Cavies

Pihas, screaming, *B 4:* 872

Pikas, *M 5:* 1200–1204, 1205–1212

Pikes, *F* **116–120**

Pilchards, *F* 73

Pileated gibbons, *M 3:* 552, 553–555, 553 (ill.), 554 (ill.)

Piliocolobus badius. See Western red colobus

Pill millipedes, *I 2:* 425, 426, 427, 429–430, 429 (ill.), 430 (ill.)

Pill woodlice, common, *CM* 178–179, 178 (ill.), 179 (ill.)

Pillbugs, *CM* **174–184**, 233, *I 2:* 239

Pilotbirds, *B 4:* 1079

Pinctada margaritifera. See Black-lipped pearl oysters

Pineapplefishes, *F* 223, 224

Pineconefishes, *F* 223, 224

Pinguinus impennis. See Great auks

Pink fairy armadillos, *M 1:* 178–179, 181, 203, 205, 209–210, 209 (ill.), 210 (ill.)

Pink river dolphins. *See* Botos

Pinnipeds. *See* Marine carnivores

Pinocchio, *M 4:* 788

Piopios, *B 5:* 1132

Pipa pipa. See Surinam toads

Pipe snakes, *R 2:* 309, 315, **320–325**, 326

Pipefishes, *F* 233, 234

Pipidae. *See* Clawed frogs; Surinam toads

Piping plovers, *B 2:* 446

Pipits, *B 4:* **924–934**

Pipra filicauda. See Wire-tailed manakins

Pipridae. *See* Manakins

Piranhas, *F* 93, 96–97, 96 (ill.), 97 (ill.)

Pirate perches, *F* 163, 164–165, 164 (ill.), 165 (ill.)

Pitangus sulphuratus. See Great kiskadees

Pithecia pithecia. See White-faced sakis

Pitheciidae. *See* Sakis; Titis; Uakaris

Pitohui kirhocephalus. See Variable pitohuis

Pitohuis, *B 4:* 1101, *B 5:* 1131
    hooded, *B 5:* 1132
    variable, *B 5:* 1136–1137, 1136 (ill.), 1137 (ill.)
    white-bellied, *B 5:* 1132

Pitta angolensis. See African pittas

Pitta sordida. See Hooded pittas

Pittas, *B 4:* **807–814**

Pitted-shell turtles. *See* Pig-nose turtles

Pittidae. *See* Pittas

Pitvipers, *R 1:* 142, *R 2:* **380–392**

Pityriasis gymnocephala. See Bornean bristleheads

Placiphorella velata. See Veiled chitons

Placozoa. *See* Placozoans

Placozoans, *CJ* **11–14**, 12 (ill.), 13 (ill.)

Plague, *M 5:* 1000

Plain chachalacas, *B 2:* 282–283, 282 (ill.), 283 (ill.)

Plain-faced bats. *See* Vespertilionid bats

Plains spadefoot toads, *A 1:* 95, 96, 98–100, 98 (ill.), 99 (ill.)

Plains viscacha rats, *M 5:* 1173

Plains viscachas, *M 5:* 1130, 1131

Plains-wanderers, *B 2:* 328, 396

Plains zebras, *M 4:* 849, 855

Planigale species, *M 1:* 56

Plantain eaters, *B 3:* **538–544**

Plantanista gangetica. See Ganges dolphins; Indus dolphins

Plantcutters, *B 4:* **881–887**

Plasmodium species, *I 2:* 340

Platanistidae. *See* Ganges dolphins; Indus dolphins

Plate-billed toucans, *B 3:* 759

Plated lizards, *R 2:* **243–248**

Platyops sterreri, CM 140

Platypus, duck-billed, *M 1:* 1–6, **15–23**, 20 (ill.), 21 (ill.)

Platypus gastric brooding frogs. *See* Northern gastric brooding frogs

Platysaurus capensis. See Cape flat lizards

Platysternidae. *See* Big-headed turtles

Platysternon megacephalum. See Big-headed turtles

Pleasing lacewings, *I 2:* 275

Plecoglossus altivelis. See Ayu

Plecoptera. *See* Stoneflies

Plectoryncha lanceolata. See Striped honeyeaters

Plectrophenax nivalis. See Snow buntings

Plectrurus perrotetii. See Nilgiri burrowing snakes

Plethodontidae. *See* Lungless salamanders

Prairie dogs, *M 5*: 998, 1015–1016, 1015 (ill.), 1016 (ill.)

Pratincoles, *B 2*: 436–443

Praying mantids, *I 1*: 189

Precocial chicks, *B 2*: 321

Prehensile-tailed hutias, *M 5*: 1188

Prehensile-tailed porcupines, *M 5*: 1126–1128, 1126 (ill.), 1127 (ill.)

Prehensile-tailed skinks, *R 2*: 253–254, 253 (ill.), 254 (ill.)

Prehensile tails, *M 3*: 527

    See also specific species

Pressure receptors, *R 1*: 104

Prey size and snakes, *R 2*: 344

Priapulans, *CJ* 167–171

Priapulida. *See* Priapulans

Priapulus caudatus, CJ 169–170, 169 (ill.), 170 (ill.)

Primates, *M 2*: 265, *M 3*: 423–427, *M 5*: 1141, 1202

Primitive blind snakes. *See* Early blind snakes

Prince Albert's lyrebirds. *See* Albert's lyrebirds

Prionops plumatus. See White helmet-shrikes

ProAvesPeru, *B 4*: 885–886

Proboscidea. *See* Elephants

Proboscis bats, *M 2*: 305, 306

Proboscis monkeys, *M 3*: 536, 537, 541–543, 541 (ill.), 542 (ill.)

Procambarus clarkii. See Red swamp crayfishes

Procavia capensis. See Rock hyraxes

Procaviidae. *See* Hyraxes

Procellaridae. *See* Fulmars; Petrels; Shearwaters

Procellariiformes. *See* Tubenosed seabirds

Procyon lotor. See Northern raccoons

Procyonidae, *M 3*: 579–580, 582, **605–613**

Proechimys semispinosus. See Spiny rats

Promerops cafer. See Cape sugarbirds

Pronghorn, *M 4*: **963–968**, 965 (ill.), 966 (ill.)

Propithecus edwardsi. See Milne-Edwards's sifakas

Proteidae. *See* Mudpuppies; Olms

Proteles cristatus. See Aardwolves

Proteocephalus longicollis, CJ 110–111, 110 (ill.), 111 (ill.)

Proteus anguinus. See Olms

Protura. *See* Proturans

Proturans, *I 1*: **45–49**, 50, 55

Prunella modularis. See Dunnocks

Prunellidae. *See* Hedge sparrows

Przewalski's horses, *M 4*: 862–863, 862 (ill.), 863 (ill.)

Psaltriparus minimus. See Bushtits

Pseudhymenochirus species. *See* Dwarf clawed frogs

Pseudis paradoxa. See Paradox frogs

Pseudo babblers, *B 5*: **1139–1144**

Pseudocheiridae. *See* Greater gliding possums; Ringtail possums

Pseudocheirus peregrinus. See Common ringtails

Pseudocolochirus violaceus. See Sea apples

Pseudoeurycea bellii. See Bell's salamanders

Pseudoscorpions, *I 1*: 17

Psittacidae. *See* Parrots

Psittaciformes. *See* Parrots

Psittacula krameri. See Rose-ringed parakeets

Psittacus erithacus. See Gray parrots

Psittirostra cantans. See Laysan finches

Psocids, *I 2*: **222–226**

Psocoptera. *See* Barklice; Book lice; Psocids

Psophia crepitans. See Common trumpeters

Psophiidae. *See* Trumpeters

Psyllophryne. See Three-toed toadlets

Ptchodera flava. See Hawaiian acorn worms

Pterocles namaqua. See Namaqua sandgrouse

Pteroclididae. *See* Sandgrouse

Pterocliformes. *See* Sandgrouse

Pterocnemia pennata. See Lesser rheas

Pterois volitans. See Red lionfishes

Pteronarcys californica. See Giant salmonflies

Pteronotus parnellii. See Parnell's moustached bats

Pterophyllum scalare. See Freshwater angelfishes

Pteropodidae. *See* Old World fruit bats

Pteropus giganteus. See Indian flying foxes

Pteropus mariannus. See Marianas fruit bats

Pterosagitta draco, CJ 237–238, 237 (ill.), 238 (ill.)

Ptilonorhynchidae. *See* Bowerbirds

Ptilonorhynchus violaceus. See Satin bowerbirds

Ptiloris victoriae. See Victoria's riflebirds

Ptyonoprogne rupestris. See Crag martins

Pubic lice, *I 2*: 230

Pudu pudu. See Southern pudus

Pudus, southern, *M 4*: 946–947, 946 (ill.), 947 (ill.)

Puerto Rican boas, *R 2*: 343

Ragfishes, F 305–307, 306
(ill.), 307 (ill.)

Rail-babblers, B 4: 1099, 1100,
1101

Rails, B 2: 315–319, 345,
356–365

Rain frogs, A 2: 325, A 3: 368,
369–370

Rainbow burrowing frogs. See
Red rain frogs

Rainbow lorikeets, B 3:
535–536, 535 (ill.), 536 (ill.)

Rainbow snakes, R 2: 400

Rainbowfishes, F 198–201

Rainforest bandicoots. See
Spiny bandicoots

Rainforests, A 2: 311, B 2: 280
See also specific species

Raja eglanteria. See Clearnose
skates

Rallidae. See Coots; Moorhens;
Rails

Ramphastidae. See Toucans

Ramphastos toco. See Toco
toucans

Ramphotyphlops nigrescens. See
Blackish blind snakes

Ramsey's pythons, R 2: 355

Rana catesbeiana. See Bullfrogs

Rana temporaria. See Brown
frogs

Rangifer tarandus. See Reindeer

Ranidae. See True frogs

Ranodon sibiricus. See
Semirechensk salamanders

Raphidae. See Dodos; Solitaires

Raphidioptera. See Snakeflies

Raphus cucullatus. See Dodos

Raptors. See Birds of prey

Raras. See Plantcutters

Raso larks, B 4: 905

Rat-kangaroos, M 1: 129–134
See also Musky rat-
kangaroos

Rat lungworms, CJ 141–142,
141 (ill.)

Rat opossums. See Shrew
opossums

Rat-tailed maggots, I 2: 337

Rat-trap fishes, F 137,
140–141, 140 (ill.), 141 (ill.)

Ratites, B 1: 1–4, 7, 12, 18,
24, 29

Rato de Taquara
Kannabateomys amblyonyx,
M 5: 1183

Rats, M 5: 996–1000,
1051–1068
cane, M 5: 1097–1102
chinchilla, M 5:
1177–1181
dassie, M 5: 1093–1096,
1094 (ill.), 1095 (ill.)
kangaroo, M 5: 997, 998,
1036–1043
plains viscacha, M 5: 1173
Polynesian, M 2: 373
rock, M 5: 1173
spiny, M 5: 1182–1187,
1185 (ill.), 1186 (ill.)
water, M 5: 998
See also Mole-rats;
Moonrats

Rattlesnakes
eastern massasauga, R 2:
381
timber, R 2: 388–389, 388
(ill.), 389 (ill.)

Ravens, B 5: 1398, 1400,
1409–1410, 1409 (ill.), 1410
(ill.)

Rays, F 9–20

Razorbills, B 2: 487

Receptors, pressure, R 1: 104

Recurvirostra americana. See
American avocets

Recurvirostridae. See Avocets;
Stilts

Red and yellow mountain
frogs, A 1: 128

Red-backed shrikes, B 4: 962

Red-backed squirrel monkeys,
M 3: 488

Red-backed toadlets, A 1: 141

Red-bellied piranhas, F 96–97,
96 (ill.), 97 (ill.)

Red-bellied turtles, Alabama, R
1: 52

Red-billed buffalo-weavers, B
5: 1307, 1308–1309

Red-billed hornbills, M 3: 638

Red-billed oxpeckers, B 5:
1334–1336, 1334 (ill.), 1335
(ill.)

Red-billed queleas, B 5: 1309

Red-billed scythebills, B 4:
833–835, 833 (ill.), 834 (ill.)

Red-billed tropicbirds, B 1:
103

Red birds of paradise, B 5:
1390

Red bishops, B 5: 1309

Red boarfishes, F 231–232,
231 (ill.), 232 (ill.)

Red-breasted cacklers. See
Gray-crowned babblers

Red-breasted nuthatches, B 5:
1176–1178, 1176 (ill.), 1177
(ill.)

Red-breasted plantcutters, B 4:
881–882, 883

Red-breasted pygmy parrots, B
3: 522

Red-browed treecreepers, B 5:
1145

Red caecilians, A 3: 517, 518,
519–520, 519 (ill.), 520 (ill.)

Red-cockaded woodpeckers, B
3: 781–783, 781 (ill.), 782
(ill.)

Red-collared widowbirds, B 5:
1306–1307

Red colobus
eastern, M 3: 537
western, M 3: 537,
538–540, 538 (ill.), 539
(ill.)

Red corals, CJ 35–36, 35 (ill.),
36 (ill.)

Red crossbills, B 5:
1285–1287, 1285 (ill.), 1286
(ill.)

Red-crowned cranes, B 2: 319,
341–342, 341 (ill.), 342 (ill.)

Rhineura floridana. See Florida wormlizards

Rhineuridae. *See* Florida wormlizards

Rhino cockroaches, *I 1:* 101

Rhinoceros iguanas, *R 1:* 169

Rhinoceros katydids, *I 1:* 168

Rhinoceros unicornis. See Indian rhinoceroses

Rhinoceroses, *M 4:* 821, 848–850, 852, 853, **874–886,** *R 1:* 71

Rhinocerotidae. *See* Rhinoceroses

Rhinocryptidae. *See* Tapaculos

Rhinoderma darwinii. See Darwin's frogs

Rhinodermatidae. *See* Vocal sac-brooding frogs

Rhinolophidae. *See* Horseshoe bats

Rhinolophus capensis. See Cape horseshoe bats

Rhinolophus ferrumequinum. See Greater horseshoe bats

Rhinophis oxyrhynchus, R 2: 315

Rhinophrynidae. *See* Mesoamerican burrowing toads

Rhinophrynus dorsalis. See Mesoamerican burrowing toads

Rhinoplax vigil. See Helmeted hornbills

Rhinopoma hardwickei. See Hardwicke's lesser mouse-tailed bats

Rhinopomatidae. *See* Mouse-tailed bats

Rhinos. *See* Rhinoceroses

Rhipidura albicollis. See White-throated fantails

Rhipidura leucophrys. See Willie wagtails

Rhipiduridae. *See* Fantails

Rhombozoa. *See* Rhombozoans

Rhombozoans, CJ 18–21

Rhopalura ophiocomae, CJ 24–25, 24 (ill.), 25 (ill.)

Rhyacotriton cascadae. See Cascade torrent salamanders

Rhyacotritonidae. *See* Torrent salamanders

Rhynchocyon cirnei. See Checkered sengis

Rhynochetidae. *See* Kagus

Rhynochetos jubatus. See Kagus

Rhyparobia maderae. See Madeira cockroaches

Ribbon snakes, northern, *R 2:* 401

Ribbon-tailed astrapias, *B 5:* 1391–1392, 1391 (ill.), 1392 (ill.)

Ribbon-tailed birds of paradise, *B 5:* 1390

Ribbon worms. *See* Anoplans; Enoplans

Rice fishes, *F* 202–203

Rice frogs. *See* Malaysian painted frogs

Richtersius coronifer. See Giant yellow water bears

Ridley seaturtles, *R 1:* 25, *26*

Riflebirds, Victoria's, *B 5:* 1393–1394, 1393 (ill.), 1394 (ill.)

Riflemen, *B 4:* 816, 817–819, 817 (ill.), 818 (ill.)

Riftia pachyptila. See Hydrothermal vent worms

Right whales, *M 4:* 783, **787–794**

See also Pygmy right whales

"Rikki-tikki-tavi" (Kipling), *M 3:* 639

The Rime of the Ancient Mariner, B 1: 46

Rimski-Korsakov, Nikolai, *I 2:* 395

Ring ouzels, *B 4:* 1015

Ring-tailed mongooses, *M 3:* 641–643, 641 (ill.), 642 (ill.)

Ringed seals, *M 3:* 594

Ringtail possums, *M 1:* **154–160**

Ringtailed lemurs, *M 3:* 451, 453–454, 453 (ill.), 454 (ill.)

Ringtails, *M 3:* 579, 605, 606
  common, *M 1:* 159–160, 159 (ill.), 160 (ill.)
  golden, *M 1:* 156
  green, *M 1:* 154
  See also Ringtail possums

Rinkhal's cobras, *R 2:* 415

Rio de Janeiro antwrens, *B 4:* 838

Riobamba marsupial frogs, **A** 2: 265–267, 265 (ill.), 266 (ill.)

River dolphins. *See* Baijis; Botos; Franciscana dolphins; Ganges dolphins; Indus dolphins

River hatchetfishes, *F* 98–99, 98 (ill.), 99 (ill.)

River horses. *See* Hippopotamuses

River-martins, white-eyed, *B 4:* 914–915

River otters, *M 3:* 614, 622

River terrapins, *R 1:* 60

River turtles
  Afro-American, *R 1:* **81–86**
  Central American, *R 1:* **39–43,** 41 (ill.), 42 (ill.)
  Eurasian, *R 1:* **58–63,** 77
  Magdalena, *R 1:* 72

River worms, *CM* 20–21, 20 (ill.), 21 (ill.)

Roadrunners, *B 3:* **545–551**

Roatelos, *B 2:* **320–325**

Robber flies, *I 2:* 336, 339

Robin accentors, *B 4:* 992

Robins, *B 4:* 1038, *B 5:* 1124
  American, *B 4:* 1014, 1015, 1022–1023, 1022 (ill.), 1023 (ill.)
  Australian, *B 5:* **1123–1129**

Rufous treecreepers, *B 5:* 1146, 1147, 1148–1150, 1148 (ill.), 1149 (ill.)

Rufous vangas, *B 4:* 976–977, 976 (ill.), 977 (ill.)

Rugiloricus cauliculus. See Bucket-tailed loriciferans

Running frogs, **A** 3: 331

Rupicola rupicola. See Guianan cocks-of-the-rock

Russet mouse lemurs, Red mouse lemurs

Russian desmans, *M 2:* 256, 257

Russian steppe cockroaches, *I 1:* 103

Rusty-belted tapaculos, *B 4:* 848–849, 848 (ill.), 849 (ill.)

Ruthven, Alexander, *A 2:* 237

Ruthven's frogs, A 2: 236–241, 238 (ill.), 239 (ill.)

Ruwenzori otter shrews, *M 2:* 233

S

Sabellaria alveolata. See Honeycomb worms

Sac-winged bats, M 2: 304–311

Saccopharyngiformes. *See* Gulpers; Swallowers

Saccopharynx ampullaceus. See Gulper eels

Saccopteryx bilineata. See Greater sac-winged bats

Saccopteryx species, *M 2:* 304, 306

Sacred ibises, *B 1:* 193, 194–195, 194 (ill.), 195 (ill.)

Sacred scarabs, *I 2:* 297, 308–309, 308 (ill.), 309 (ill.)

Saddleback toads. *See Brachycephalus nodoterga*

Saddlebacks (Birds), *B 5:* 1353, 1354, 1355

Saffron-bellied frogs, *A 3:* 368, 373

Saffron toucanets, *B 3:* 759

Sagittariidae. *See* Secretary birds

Sagittarius serpentarius. See Secretary birds

Saguinus oedipus. See Cotton-top tamarins

Saimiri sciureus. See Common squirrel monkeys

Saintpaulia species, *I 2:* 439–440

Sakis, M 3: 516–525

Salamanders, A 3: 398–402
amphiumas, A 3: 494–500
Asiatic, A 3: 409–418
Asiatic giant, A 3: 419–426
dwarf sirens, A 3: 403–408
European, A 3: 440–460
hellbenders, A 3: 419–426, 423 (ill.), 424 (ill.)
lungless, A 3: 476–493
mole, A 3: 433–439
mudpuppies, A 3: 461–470, 467 (ill.), 468 (ill.)
newts, A 3: 440–460
olms, A 3: 461–470, 465 (ill.), 466 (ill.)
Pacific giant, A 3: 427–432
sirens, A 3: 403–408
torrent, A 3: 471–475

Salamandra salamandra. See European fire salamanders

Salamandridae. *See* European salamanders; Newts

Salim Ali's fruit bats, *M 2:* 315

Salinella, CJ 15–17

Salinella salve, CJ 15–17, 16 (ill.), 17 (ill.)

Salmo salar. See Atlantic salmons

Salmon lice, *CM* 228–229, 228 (ill.), 229 (ill.)

Salmonflies, giant, *I 1:* 96–97, 96 (ill.), 97 (ill.)

Salmoniformes. *See* Salmons

Salmons, F 127–135

Salps, CJ 257–262, 261 (ill.)

Salt-desert cavies, *M 5:* 1139, 1140

Salticus scenicus. See Zebra jumping spiders

Saltopus species, *R 1:* 2–3

Salvelinus fontinalis. See Brook trouts

San Clemente loggerhead shrikes, *B 4:* 970

San Francisco garter snakes, *R 2:* 406

San Joaquin pocket mice, *M 5:* 1039–1040, 1039 (ill.), 1040 (ill.)

Sanaga pygmy herrings, *F* 73

Sand boas, *R 2:* 342, 343, 344

Sand dollars, CJ 206, **212–224**

Sand fiddler crabs, *CM* 133–134, 133 (ill.), 134 (ill.)

Sand flies, *I 2:* 340

Sand frogs, *A 1:* 124

Sand isopods, *CM* 180–181, 180 (ill.), 181 (ill.)

Sand lances, inshore, *F* 294–295, 294 (ill.), 295 (ill.)

Sand lizards, *R 2:* 222, 225–226, 225 (ill.), 226 (ill.)

Sand monitors, *R 2:* 280

Sand puppies. *See* Naked mole-rats

Sand skinks, *R 2:* 252

Sand stars, *CJ* 188, 190–191, 190 (ill.), 191 (ill.)

Sand swimmers. *See* Yellow golden moles

Sand worms, CM 1–11

Sanders, Howard, *CM* 72

Sanderson's hook frogs, *A 2:* 290–291

Sandfish, *F* 79, 80, *R 2:* 257–258, 257 (ill.), 258 (ill.)

Sclater's larks, *B 4:* 905

Scleroglossa, *R 2:* 273

Sclerophyll forests, *B 4:* 1095

Scolecomorphidae. *See* Buried-eyed caecilians

Scolecomorphus kirkii. See Kirk's caecilians

Scoliid wasps, *I 2:* 393

Scolopacidae. *See* Sandpipers

Scolopenders, *I 2:* 417, 419–420, 419 (ill.), 420 (ill.)

Scolopendra abnormis. See Serpent Island centipedes

Scolopendra morsitans. See Scolopenders

Scombroidei, F 334–342

Scopidae. *See* Hammerheads

Scopus umbretta. See Hammerheads

Scorpaeniformes, F 247–255

Scorpionfishes, F 247–255

Scorpionflies, I 2: 320–326

Scorpions, I 1: 9, **15–44,** *I 2:* 238

Scotoplanes globosa. See Sea pigs

Screamers, *B 2:* 241–245, **261–265**

Screaming cowbirds, *B 5:* 1276

Screaming pihas, *B 4:* 872

Screech-owls, *B 3:* 553, 567–569, 567 (ill.), 568 (ill.)

Scrub-birds, *B 4:* **895–900,** *B 5:* 1146

Scrub-jays, western, *B 5:* 1403–1404, 1403 (ill.), 1404 (ill.)

Scrub robins, *B 5:* 1123, 1127–1128 (ill.), 1127 (ill.), 1128 (ill.)

Sculpins, *F 247–249*

Scutes, *R 1:* 51

Scutigera coleoptrata. See House centipedes

Scutigerella immaculata. See Garden symphylans

Scutigerella species, *I 2:* 435

Scyphozoa. *See* Jellyfish

Scythebills
    greater, *B 4:* 832
    red-billed, *B 4:* 833–835, 833 (ill.), 834 (ill.)

Sea apples, *CJ* 230–231, 230 (ill.), 231 (ill.)

Sea catfishes, *F 102*

Sea cows, *M 4:* 828–832, **833–840**

Sea cucumbers, *CJ 206,* **225–234,** *CM 243, F 168*

Sea daisies, *CJ 200–204,* 206

Sea eagles, *B 1:* 212

Sea kraits, *R 1:* 140, *R 2:* 416, 425–426, 425 (ill.), 426 (ill.)

Sea lampreys, *F 7–8,* 7 (ill.), 8 (ill.)

Sea lilies, *CJ 181–187,* 206

Sea lions, *M 3:* 581, 582, **673–683,** *M 4:* 707

Sea mats, *CM 314–315,* 314 (ill.), 315 (ill.)

Sea minks, *M 3:* 581

Sea monkeys, *CM 78*

Sea nettles, *CJ 60–61,* 60 (ill.), 61 (ill.)

Sea otters, *M 3:* 579, 582, 614, *M 4:* 707

Sea pigs, *CJ* 232–233, 232 (ill.), 233 (ill.)

Sea scorpions, *I 1:* 9

Sea skaters, *I 2:* 237, 252–253, 252 (ill.), 253 (ill.)

Sea slugs, CM 260–273

Sea snakes, *R 2:* **414–426**

Sea spiders, I 1: 1–7

Sea squirts, CJ 248–256

Sea stars, *CJ* **187–200,** 206

Sea urchins, *CJ* 206, **212–224,** *F 318*

Sea walnuts, *CJ 71–72,* 71 (ill.), 72 (ill.)

Sea wasps, *CJ* 54, 55–56, 55 (ill.), 56 (ill.)

Seabirds, *B 1:* 101

Seadragons, leafy, *F* 237–238, 237 (ill.), 238 (ill.)

Seahorses, F 233–241

Seals, *M 4:* 707
    crab-eater, *M 3:* 580
    eared, *M 3:* 579, 582, **673–683,** 690
    elephant, *M 3:* 578, 684, 691, 695–697, 695 (ill.), 696 (ill.)
    fur, *M 3:* **673–683**
    monk, *M 3:* 581, 582, 691, 698–700, 698 (ill.), 699 (ill.)
    ringed, *M 3:* 594
    true, *M 3:* 579, 582, **690–701**

Seaturtles, *R 1:* **24–32**
    See also Leatherback seaturtles

Secernentea. *See* Secernenteans

Secernenteans, *CJ* **137–142**

Secretary birds, *B 1:* 207, **223–228,** 225 (ill.), 226 (ill.)

Sedillo Spring, *CM 176*

Seed-eaters, *B 5:* 1288
    See also specific species

Seedsnipes, *B 2:* 396, **464–468**

Sei whales, *M 4:* 797

Seismosaurus species, *R 1:* 2

Seison nebaliae, CJ 120–121, 120 (ill.), 121 (ill.)

Self-anointing behavior, *M 2:* 220

Semibalanus balanoides. See Rock barnacles

Semirechensk salamanders, **A 3:** 411, 417–418, 417 (ill.), 418 (ill.)

Semnornis ramphastinus. See Toucan barbets

Semper's warblers, *B 5:* 1260

Senegal bushbabies, *M 3:* 424, 437, 439–440, 439 (ill.), 440 (ill.)

Senegal running frogs. *See* Bubbling kassinas

Senegal thick-knees, *B 2*: 431

Sengis, *M 5*: **1223–1228**

Sequential polyandry, *B 2*: 327

Seriemas, *B 2*: 316, 317, 318, **382–386**

Serows, *M 4*: 983–984, 983 (ill.), 984 (ill.)

Serpent Island centipedes, *I 2*: 418

Serpula vermicularis. See Tubeworms

Setae, *R 1*: 179

Seventeen-year cicadas, *I 2*: 245–247, 245 (ill.), 246 (ill.)

Sewellels. *See* Mountain beavers

Sex differentiation, echiurans, *CM* 52

Seychelles frogs, *A 1*: **117–123**, 121 (ill.), 122 (ill.)

Seychelles mud turtles, *R 1*: 72

Seychelles palm frogs, *A 1*: 117, 119

Seychelles sunbirds, *B 5*: 1208

Seychelles swiftlets, *B 3*: 617

Seychelles treefrogs, *A 3*: 332, 336

Shads, *F* 73

Shakespeare, William, *B 3*: 555, *B 5*: 1327, *M 2*: 248

Shanks, *B 2*: 454

Shark Bay, Australia, *M 4*: 834

Sharks, *CM* 222, *F* **9–20**, *M 4*: 834

Sharp-nosed reed frogs, *A 3*: 334, 335–336

Sharp-tailed sandpipers, *B 2*: 455

Sharpbills, *B 4*: **860–863**, 862 (ill.), 863 (ill.)

Shearwaters, *B 1*: 43, **53–60**

Sheath-tailed bats, *M 2*: **304–311**

Sheathbills, *B 2*: 396, **469–474**

Sheep, *M 4*: 888, 890, **969–987**

Sheep and goat fleas, *I 2*: 333–334, 333 (ill.), 334 (ill.)

Shellac, *I 2*: 240

Shells, *CM* 263, 290

Shepherd's beaked whales, *M 4*: 749, 755–756, 755 (ill.), 756 (ill.)

Shield limpets, *CM* 268–269, 268 (ill.), 269 (ill.)

Shieldbacks, Antioch dunes, *I 1*: 171

Shieldtail snakes, *R 2*: **314–319**

Shillong bubble-nest frogs, *A 3*: 356

Shinisauridae, *R 2*: 269

Shiny woodlice, common, *CM* 182–183, 182 (ill.), 183 (ill.)

Shipworms, *CM* 276

Shoebills, *B 1*: 143, 145, **186–191**, 188 (ill.), 189 (ill.)

Shore plovers, *B 2*: 445, 446

Shorebirds. *See* Charadriiformes

Short-beaked echidnas, *M 1*: 2–3, 5, 7–8, 9, 11–13, 11 (ill.), 12 (ill.)

Short-eared owls, *B 3*: 554

Short-faced scorpionflies, *I 2*: 322

Short-headed wormlizards. *See* Spade-headed wormlizards

Short-horned lizards, *R 1*: 169

Short-nose sturgeons, *F* 34

Short-nosed echidnas. *See* Short-beaked echidnas

Short-tailed bats, New Zealand, *M 2*: **371–377**

Short-tailed chinchillas, *M 5*: 1131

Short-tailed opossums, gray, *M 1*: 28

Short-tailed shrews, *M 2*: 247, 248

Shovel-billed kingfishers, *B 3*: 655

Shovel-nosed frogs, *A 2*: **323–329**

Shovel-snouted lizards, *R 2*: 222

Shrew moles, *M 2*: **255–262**

Shrew opossums, *M 1*: **37–43**

Shrews, *M 2*: 213–214, 215, 216, **246–254**

  otter, *M 2*: 232, 233, 234

  tree, *M 2*: **263–268**, 1202, *M 5*: 1224

  true, *M 1*: 37, *M 5*: 1224

  See also Sengis

Shrike-thrushes, *B 5*: 1131, 1132

Shrike-tits, *B 5*: 1131

Shrikes, *B 4*: 790–791, **962–971**

  See also Cuckoo-shrikes; Magpie-shrikes

Shrimps, *CM* **121–137**

  clam, *CM* **75–86**

  coral, *CM* 119

  fairy, *CM* **75–86**

  glass, *CM* 141–142, 141 (ill.), 142 (ill.)

  Great Lake, *CM* 106

  mantis, *CM* **92–99**

  mussel, *CM* **231–236**

  skeleton, *CM* 188–189, 188 (ill.), 189 (ill.)

  snapping, *CM* 119

  tadpole, *CM* **75–86**

Sialia sialis. See Eastern bluebirds

Siamangs, *M 3*: 552, 559–561, 559 (ill.), 560 (ill.)

Siamese fighting fishes, *F* 351–352, 351 (ill.), 352 (ill.)

Siberian accentors, *B 4*: 992

Siberian cranes, *B 2*: 319, 334

Siberian musk deer, *M 4*: 935–936, 935 (ill.), 936 (ill.)

Siberian pikas. *See* Northern pikas

Siberian salamanders, *A 3*: 411

Siboglinum fiordicum. See Norwegian tubeworms

Sickle-billed vangas, *B 4:* 972, 973

Sicklebills, *B 5:* 1390

Sidamo bushlarks, *B 4:* 905

Side-necked turtles, *R 1:* 9, 10, 14, 77

    African, *R 1:* 70–75, 81

    Australo-American, *R 1:* 18–23

    See also Afro-American river turtles

Side-stabbing snakes. *See* Southern burrowing asps

Sifakas, *M 3:* 425, **458–465**

Sigmodon hispidus. See Hispid cotton rats

Silk, spider, *I 1:* 17

Silkworms, *I 2:* 372, 374–375, 374 (ill.), 375 (ill.)

Silky anteaters, *M 1:* 179, 180, 195, 196, 198–199, 198 (ill.), 199 (ill.)

Silky flycatchers, *B 4:* **979–987**

Silky lacewings, *I 2:* 275

Silky shrew opossums, *M 1:* 38–39, 40, 41–42, 41 (ill.), 42 (ill.)

Silky tuco-tucos, *M 5:* 1167

Silurana tropicalis. See Tropical clawed frogs

Siluriformes. *See* Catfishes

Silver carps, *F* 88–89, 88 (ill.), 89 (ill.)

Silverbacks, *M 3:* 564, 568

Silverfish, *I 1:* 61, **65–70,** 67 (ill.), 68 (ill.)

Silversides, *F* **198–201**

Simony's giant lizards, *R 2:* 223

Sinentomon yoroi, I 1: 48–49, 48 (ill.), 49 (ill.)

Singleslits, *F* **308–312**

Siphonaptera. *See* Fleas

Sipuncula. *See* Peanut worms

Sipunculus nudus, CM 48, 48 (ill.)

Siren intermedia. See Lesser sirens

Sirenia, *M 4:* **828–832**

Sirenidae. *See* Dwarf sirens; Sirens

Sirens, *A 3:* **403–408**

Sitta canadensis. See Red-breasted nuthatches

Sitta europaea. See Nuthatches

Sittellas, *B 5:* 1173

Sittidae. *See* Nuthatches; Wall creepers

Six keyhole sand dollars, *CJ* 221–222, 221 (ill.), 222 (ill.)

Six-lined racerunners, *R 2:* 237, 238–239, 238 (ill.), 239 (ill.)

Skates, *F* **9–20**

Skeins, *B 2:* 253

Skeleton shrimps, *CM* 188–189, 188 (ill.), 189 (ill.)

Skeletons, of priapulans, *CJ* 168

Skimmers, *B 2:* 475–477

Skin, shedding, *R 2:* 304, 376

Skin beetles, *I 2:* 293

Skinks, *R 2:* **249–259**

    See also Blindskinks

Skinnycheek lanternfishes, *F* 151–152, 151 (ill.), 152 (ill.)

Skippers, *I 2:* **366–389**

Skuas, *B 2:* 475–477, 479–480 (ill.), 479 (ill.), 480 (ill.)

Skunk frogs, *A 2:* 224

Skunks, *M 3:* 578, 579, **614–627,** 637

Skylarks, *B 4:* 904

Slaters, *CM* **174–184,** 233

Sleep, dolphins, *M 4:* 720

Slender-billed curlews, *B 2:* 456

Slender-billed grackles, *B 5:* 1269

Slender blind snakes, *R 1:* 140, *R 2:* 288–289, **295–301,** 402

Slender giant morays, *F* 66–67, 66 (ill.), 67 (ill.)

Slender gray lorises, *M 3:* 428

Slender lorises, *M 3:* 428–429

Slender mud frogs, *A 1:* 77

Slender pigeon lice, *I 2:* 234–235, 234 (ill.), 235 (ill.)

Slime and hagfishes, *F 2*

Slit-faced bats, *M 2:* **316–322**

Sloth bears, *M 3:* 593, 594, 595

Sloth lemurs, *M 3:* 459

Sloths, *M 1:* **178–182**

    three-toed tree, *M 1:* 178, 181, **189–194**

    two-toed tree, *M 1:* 178, 180, **183–188**

    West Indian, *M 1:* **183–188**

Slow lorises, *M 3:* 428

Slowworms, *R 2:* 260, 262

Slugs, sea, CM 260–273

Small bog turtles, *R 1:* 50

Small buttonquails, *B 2:* 329–330, 329 (ill.), 330 (ill.)

Small-eared galagos. *See* Northern greater bushbabies

Small-eared shrews, *M 2:* 247

Small mouse-tailed bats, *M 2:* 299

Small Sulawesi cuscuses, *M 1:* 116

Small-webbed bell toads, *A 1:* 29

Smasher shrimps, *CM* 94, 95

Smelts, *F* **121–126**

Sminthurus viridis. See Lucerne fleas

Smith, Doug, *B 2:* 268

Smith, Nancy, *B 2:* 289

Smithornis capensis. See African broadbills

Smoky bats, *M 2:* **383–387,** 385 (ill.), 386 (ill.)

Smooth newts, *A 3:* 445–446, 445 (ill.), 446 (ill.)

Smooth-scaled splitjaw snakes, *R 2:* 363–367

Smooth-tailed tree shrews, Bornean, *M 2:* 265

Sorberaceans, CJ 267–270

Sorex palustris. See American water shrews

Soricidae. *See* Shrews

South African ostriches, B 1: 35

South African porcupines, M 5: 1117–1119, 1117 (ill.), 1118 (ill.)

South American beavers. *See* Coypus

South American blind snakes, R 2: 291

South American bullfrogs, A 2: 155, 170–172, 170 (ill.), 171 (ill.)

South American knifefishes, F 109–115

South American lungfishes, F 25–26, 25 (ill.), 26 (ill.)

South American mice, M 5: 1051, 1052

South American painted snipes, B 2: 407, 408

South American pearl kites, B 1: 212

South American rats, M 5: 1051, 1052

South American river turtles, R 1: 82, 84–86, 84 (ill.), 85 (ill.)

South Georgian diving-petrels, B 1: 67

South Island kokakos, B 5: 1356

South Island saddlebacks, B 5: 1355

Southeast Asian flying snakes, R 2: 400

Southern bromeliad woodsnakes, R 2: 372–373, 372 (ill.), 373 (ill.)

Southern brown bandicoots, M 1: 76, 80

Southern burrowing asps, R 2: 396–397, 396 (ill.), 397 (ill.)

Southern cassowaries, B 1: 19, 20, 21–23, 21 (ill.), 22 (ill.)

Southern cod-icefishes, F 288–291

Southern day frogs. *See* Mount Glorious day frogs

Southern dibblers, M 1: 54

Southern elephant seals, M 3: 578

Southern flying squirrels, M 5: 1011–1012, 1011 (ill.), 1012 (ill.)

Southern gastric brooding frogs, A 1: 143

Southern ground-hornbills, B 3: 653–654, 717–719, 717 (ill.), 718 (ill.)

Southern hairy-nosed wombats, M 1: 103, 111, 112

Southern house wrens, B 4: 1039

Southern logrunners, B 4: 1093, 1094–1095, 1096–1098, 1096 (ill.), 1097 (ill.)

Southern marsupial moles, M 1: 96, 97–98, 97 (ill.), 98 (ill.)

Southern muriquis, M 3: 527

Southern opossums, M 1: 28

Southern pudus, M 4: 946–947, 946 (ill.), 947 (ill.)

Southern red bishops, B 5: 1315–1316, 1315 (ill.), 1316 (ill.)

Southern scrub robins, B 5: 1127–1128, 1127 (ill.), 1128 (ill.)

Southern tamanduas, M 1: 179, 195

Southern three-toed toadlets, A 2: 190

Southern tokoeka kiwis, B 1: 32, 33

Southern tree hyraxes, M 4: 823–824, 823 (ill.), 824 (ill.)

Southern two-toed sloths. *See* Linné's two-toed sloths

Southwestern blind snakes. *See* Western blind snakes

Southwestern toads. *See* Arroyo toads

Sowbugs, I 2: 239

Space, frogs in, A 1: 63

Spade-headed wormlizards, R 1: 191, 204, 208–213

Spadefoot toads, A 1: 94–101

Spaghetti worms, CJ 246–247, 246 (ill.), 247 (ill.)

Spangled cotingas, B 4: 875–876, 875 (ill.), 876 (ill.)

Spangled drongos, B 5: 1346

Sparkling violet-ears, B 3: 634–635, 634 (ill.), 635 (ill.)

Sparrow-larks, B 4: 903, 904

Sparrowhawks, B 5: 1346

Sparrows, B 5: 1318–1325
   hedge, **B 4: 991–996**
   Java, B 5: 1298
   savanna, B 5: 1255–1257, 1255 (ill.), 1256 (ill.)
   song, B 5: 1247–1249, 1247 (ill.), 1248 (ill.)

Spea bombifrons. See Plains spadefoot toads

Spearer shrimps, CM 94

Species,
   endangered, A 1: 4, R 2: 238
      introduced, A 1: 4, 48–49, A 2: 157, CM 106, 276, 280–281, M 1: 65, R 2: 370
      invasive, F 354
      relict, R 2: 332
      scientific names of, F 257, R 2: 321
      super, A 3: 336
      taxonomy and, F 257
      See also specific species

Speckled cats. *See* Bowfins

Spectacled bears, M 3: 593, 594, 595

Spectacled caimans. *See* Common caimans

Spectacled porpoises, *M 4:* 729–730, 731

Spectral vampire bats, *M 2:* 345, 347

Spectres, Macleay's, *I 1:* 205–207, 205 (ill.), 206 (ill.)

Spelaeogriphacea. *See* Spelaeogriphaceans

Spelaeogriphaceans, CM 165–169

Spelaeogriphus lepidops, CM 166, 167–168, 167 (ill.), 168 (ill.)

Speleonectes gironensis, CM 68–69, 68 (ill.), 69 (ill.)

Speleonectes lucayensis, CM 67

Spencer's burrowing frogs, **A** *1:* 124, 126

Sperm whale lice, *CM* 190–191, 190 (ill.), 191 (ill.)

Sperm whales, M 4: 758–766, 761 (ill.), 762 (ill.)

Spermaceti, *M 4:* 759

Sphagnum frogs, *A 1:* 128

Sphecotheres vieilloti. See Australasian figbirds

Spheniscidae. *See* Penguins

Sphenisciformes. *See* Penguins

Spheniscus magellanicus. See Magellanic penguins

Sphenodon punctatus. See Tuataras

Sphenodontidae. *See* Tuataras

Sphyraena barracuda. See Great barracudas

Sphyrapicus varius. See Yellow-bellied sapsuckers

Spider bat flies, *I 2:* 348–349, 348 (ill.), 349 (ill.)

Spider crabs, Japanese, *CM* 121

Spider monkeys, M 3: 425, **526–535**

Spider webs, *I 1:* 17

Spiderhunters, *B 5:* 1209

Spiders, I 1: 15–44

See also Sea spiders

Spine-tailed logrunners. *See* Southern logrunners

Spinejaw snakes, R 2: 369–374

Spinner dolphins, *M 4:* 706, 746–747, 746 (ill.), 747 (ill.)

Spinosaurus species, *R 1:* 2

Spiny agamas, *R 1:* 148–149, 148 (ill.), 149 (ill.)

Spiny anteaters. *See* Echidnas

Spiny bandicoots, M 1: 74, 75, **88–93**

Spiny eels, F 55–56, **242–246**

Spiny-headed treefrogs, *A 2:* 262, 263

Spiny-knee leaf frogs, *A 2:* 264

Spiny leaf-folding frogs. *See* Greater leaf-folding frogs

Spiny lobsters, Caribbean, *CM* 123

Spiny mice, Egyptian, *M 5:* 1060–1061, 1060 (ill.), 1061 (ill.)

Spiny rats, M 5: 1182–1187, 1185 (ill.), 1186 (ill.)

Spiny softshells, *R 1:* 98–100, 98 (ill.), 99 (ill.)

Spiny-tailed lizards, Dabb, *R 1:* 146

Spinytail iguanas, cape, *R 1:* 170–171, 170 (ill.), 171 (ill.)

Spiomenia spiculata, CM 245–246, 245 (ill.), 246 (ill.)

Spiracles, *A 1:* 57

Spirit owls. *See* Barn owls

Spirobolus species, *I 2:* 428

Spix's disk-winged bats, *M 2:* 391–393, 391 (ill.), 392 (ill.)

Spix's saddleback toads. *See* Pumpkin toadlets

Splendid fairy-wrens, *B 4:* 1073–1075, 1073 (ill.), 1074 (ill.)

Splendid poison frogs, *A 2:* 225

Split-footed lacewings, *I 2:* 276

Splitfin flashlightfishes, *F* 225–226, 225 (ill.), 226 (ill.)

Splitjaw snakes, R 2: **363–368,** 366 (ill.), 367 (ill.)

Sponges, CJ 1–11

Spongilla flies, *I 2:* 274, 275

Spongilla lacustris. See Freshwater sponges

Spoon-billed sandpipers, *B 2:* 456

Spoon worms. *See* Echiurans

Spoonbills, B 1: 144, 145, 147, **192–199**

Spoonwing lacewings, *I 2:* 273, 274, 275, 286–288, 286 (ill.), 287 (ill.)

Sportive lemurs, M 3: **466–471**

Spot-billed pelicans, *B 1:* 135

Spotted-back weavers. *See* Village weavers

Spotted bowerbirds, *B 5:* 1386–1388, 1386 (ill.), 1387 (ill.)

Spotted buttonquails, *B 2:* 328

Spotted flycatchers, *B 4:* 1061, 1063–1064, 1063 (ill.), 1064 (ill.)

Spotted gars, *F* 39–40, 39 (ill.), 40 (ill.)

Spotted greenbuls, *B 4:* 944

Spotted hyenas, *M 3:* 649, 650, 651–653, 651 (ill.), 652 (ill.)

Spotted lazy toads, *A 1:* 80

Spotted marsh frogs, *A 1:* 127

Spotted munias, *B 5:* 1303–1304, 1303 (ill.), 1304 (ill.)

Spotted nutcrackers, *B 5:* 1407–1408, 1407 (ill.), 1408 (ill.)

Spotted owls, *B 3:* 555

Spotted quail-thrushes, *B 4:* 1100, 1101, 1102–1104, 1102 (ill.), 1103 (ill.)

Spotted ratfishes, *F* 11–12, 11 (ill.), 12 (ill.)

Spotted sandpipers, *B 2:* 455

Spotted snout-burrowers, **A** 2: 323–324, 326

Spotted-tailed quolls, *M 1:* 52

Spotted tobies, *F* 372–373, 372 (ill.), 373 (ill.)

Sprague, Isaac, *B 4:* 933

Sprague's pipits, *B 4:* 932–933, 932 (ill.), 933 (ill.)

Sprats, *F* 73

Spread adders. *See* Eastern hog-nosed snakes

Spreadwings, *I 1:* 82

Spring lizards. *See* Salamanders

Spring peeper frogs, *A 1:* 4

Springhares, M 5: 1076–1080, 1078 (ill.), 1079 (ill.)

Springtails, I 1: 45, **50–54,** 55

Squamata. *See* Lizards; Snakes

Square-tailed drongos, *B 5:* 1348–1349, 1348 (ill.), 1349 (ill.)

Squarehead catfishes, *F* 105–106, 105 (ill.), 106 (ill.)

Squeakers, A 2: 310–322

Squids, CM 293–305

Squilla mantis, CM 95

Squirrel gliders, *M 1:* 163

Squirrel monkeys, M 3: 424, 487–495

Squirrelfishes, F 223–228

Squirrels, M 5: 996, 998, **1008–1021**

> *See also* Scaly-tailed squirrels

St. Helena earwigs, *I 1:* 160, 163–164, 163 (ill.), 164 (ill.)

St. Helena plovers, *B 2:* 446

Stable flies, *I 2:* 336

Stag beetles, *I 2:* 294, 303–305, 303 (ill.), 304 (ill.)

Stalk-eyed flies, *I 2:* 344–345, 344 (ill.), 345 (ill.)

Star-nosed moles, *M 2:* 214, 260–261, 260 (ill.), 261 (ill.)

Stargazers, northern, *F* 296–297, 296 (ill.), 297 (ill.)

Starlings, B 5: 1269, **1326–1336**

Steamer-ducks, *B 2:* 241

Steatornis caripensis. See Oilbirds

Steatornithidae. *See* Oilbirds

Stegosaurs, *R 1:* 2

Steindachner's turtles, *R 1:* 19

Steller, Georg Wilhelm, *M 4:* 834, 835

Steller sea lions, *M 3:* 674

Steller's sea cows, *M 4:* 828, 830–831, 833–834, 835, 836–837, 836 (ill.), 837 (ill.)

Stenella longirostris. See Spinner dolphins

Stephanoberyciformes, F 219–222

Stephen's rocket frogs, *A 2:* 219, 222

Steppe pikas, *M 5:* 1205–1206

Stercorarius parasiticus. See Arctic skuas

Sternotherus odoratus. See Stinkpots

Stewart Island brown kiwis. *See* Haast tokoeka kiwis

Stick insects, I 1: 158, **193–210**

Sticklebacks, F 233–241

Stiltia isabella. See Australian pratincoles

Stilts, B 2: 423–430

Stink bugs, *I 2:* 240

Stink fights, *M 3:* 451

Stinking pheasants. *See* Hoatzins

Stinkpots, *R 1:* 67–69, 67 (ill.), 68 (ill.)

Stoker, Bram, *M 2:* 279, 346

Stomatopoda. *See* Mantis shrimps

Stomiiformes, F 136–141

Stone centipedes, *I 2:* 417

Stone-curlews, *B 2:* 432, 433

Stonechats, *B 4:* 1020–1021, 1020 (ill.), 1021 (ill.)

Stoneflies, I 1: 92–98

Stonemason toadlets, *A 1:* 140

Stonerollers, *F* 86–87, 86 (ill.), 87 (ill.)

Storks, B 1: 143–146, **166–174,** 175, 186, 187

Storm-petrels, B 1: 41, **61–66**

Storm's storks, *B 1:* 166

Stout beardfishes, *F* 160–161, 160 (ill.), 161 (ill.)

Stout infantfishes, *F* 318

Stranded whales, *M 4:* 751

Stratum corneum, *R 2:* 304

Strawberry poison frogs, **A** 2: 218–219, 221–224

Streak-breasted bulbuls, *B 4:* 946

Streaked cisticolas. *See* Zitting cisticolas

Strepsiptera. *See* Twisted-wing parasites

Streseman's bristlefronts, *B 4:* 847

Striated bulbuls, *B 4:* 944

Striated grasswrens, *B 4:* 1076–1077, 1076 (ill.), 1077 (ill.)

Striated pardalotes, *B 5:* 1205–1207, 1205 (ill.), 1206 (ill.)

Strigidae. *See* Typical owls

Strigiformes. *See* Owls

Stripe-breasted rhabdornis, *B 5:* 1188, 1190

Stripe-headed rhabdornis, *B 5:* 1188, 1190, 1191–1193, 1191 (ill.), 1192 (ill.)

Stripe-necked turtles, Chinese, *R 1:* 59

Stripe-sided rhabdornis. *See* Stripe-headed rhabdornis

Striped bandicoots. *See* Eastern barred bandicoots

Striped honeyeaters, *B 5:* 1233–1234, 1233 (ill.), 1234 (ill.)

Striped hyenas, *M 3:* 649–650

Striped parrotfishes, *F* 277–278, 277 (ill.), 278 (ill.)

Striped poison-fang blennies, *F* 301–302, 301 (ill.), 302 (ill.)

Striped possums, M 1: 161–166

Striped skunks, *M 3:* 619–621, 619 (ill.), 620 (ill.)

Striped snakeheads, *F* 355–356, 355 (ill.), 356 (ill.)

Striped snakes, *R 1:* 141

Stripes, zebras, *M 4:* 855

Stromateoidei, F 343–346

Strongylura exilis. See Californian needlefishes

Strophidon sathete. See Slender giant morays

Struthio camelus. See Ostriches

Struthionidae. *See* Ostriches

Struthioniformes, B 1: 1–4

Stupendemys geographicus, R 1: 82

Sturgeons, F 32–36

Sturnidae. *See* Mynas; Starlings

Sturnus vulgaris. See European starlings

Stygiomysis cokei, CM 143–144, 143 (ill.), 144 (ill.)

Stygobromus hayi, CM 186

Stylochus inimicus. See Oyster leeches

Subdesert mesites, *B 2:* 320, 321

Sucker-footed bats, Old World, M 2: 389, 395–398, 397 (ill.)

See also Disk-winged bats

Sucking lice, I 2: 227–235

Sugar gliders, *M 1:* 163, 164–166, 164 (ill.), 165 (ill.)

Sugarbirds, Cape, *B 5:* 1231–1232, 1231 (ill.), 1232 (ill.)

Sugarfoot moth flies, *I 2:* 341

Suidae. *See* Pigs

Sula nebouxii. See Blue-footed boobies

Sulawesi bear cuscuses, *M 1:* 116, 117

Sulawesi palm civets, *M 3:* 630

Sulawesi red-knobbed hornbills, *B 3:* 722–724, 722 (ill.), 723 (ill.)

Sulidae. *See* Boobies; Gannets

Sumaco horned treefrogs, *A 2:* 261, 268–270, 268 (ill.), 269 (ill.)

Sumatran blue-masked leafbirds, *B 4:* 957

Sumatran orangutans, *M 3:* 426

Sumatran rhinoceroses, *M 4:* 850, 875, 876, 877–879, 877 (ill.), 878 (ill.)

Sumba buttonquails, *B 2:* 328

Sumba hawk owls, *B 3:* 565

Sun bears, Malaysian, *M 3:* 593, 594

Sun spiders, *I 1:* 15, 17

Sunbeam snakes, R 2: 331–336

See also Neotropical sunbeam snakes

Sunbirds, B 5: 1208–1217

See also False sunbirds

Sunbitterns, B 2: 315, 316, 318, **372–375,** 374 (ill.), 375 (ill.)

Sungrebes, B 2: 316, 317, **366–371,** 369 (ill.), 370 (ill.)

Sunset frogs, *A 1:* 139

Supella longipalpa. See Brownbanded cockroaches

Super species, *A 3:* 336

Superb Australian fairy-wrens, *B 4:* 1071

Superb lyrebirds, *B 4:* 888–890

Surface-to-volume ration and moisture, *R 2:* 297

Surfperches, F 272–280

Surgeonfishes, F 326–333

Surinam horned frogs, **A** 2: 155, 158–160, 158 (ill.), 159 (ill.)

Surinam toads, A 1: 62–76, 73–75, 73 (ill.), 74 (ill.)

Sus scrofa. See Eurasian wild pigs

Swallowers, F 68–69

Swallows, B 4: 789, 790, **913–923**

See also Woodswallows

Swallowtail butterflies, *I 2:* 368

Swamp eels, F 242–246

Swamp greenbuls, *B 4:* 945–946

Swans, B 2: 241–245, **246–260**

Swiftlets, *B 3:* 612, 614

Aitu, *B 3:* 617

cave, *B 3:* 613, 616

Guam, *B 3:* 617

Swifts, B 3: 610–614, 612–613, **615–623, 624–629**

See also Tree swifts

Swordtails, green, *F* 214–215, 214 (ill.), 215 (ill.)

Sylvestri, Antonio, *I 1:* 46

Sylviidae. *See* Old World warblers

Sylvilagus audubonii. See Desert cottontails

Symphalangus syndactylus. See Siamangs

Symphyla. *See* Symphylans

Symphylans, I 2: 434–437

Synbranchiformes. *See* Spiny eels; Swamp eels

Synbranchus marmoratus. See Marbled swamp eels

Synthetic sponges, *CJ* 2

Syrrhaptes paradoxus. See Pallas's sandgrouse

T

Tabanus punctifer. See Big black horse flies

Table Mountain, South Africa, *CM* 166, 167–168

Table Mountain ghost frogs. *See* Rose's ghost frogs

Tacarcula tapaculos, *B 4:* 847

Tachycines asynamorus. See Greenhouse camel crickets

Tachyglossidae. *See* Echidnas

Tachyglossus aculeatus. See Short-beaked echidnas

Taczanowski's tinamous, *B 1:* 7

Tadarida brasiliensis. See Brazilian free-tailed bats

Tadpole shrimps, CM 75–86

Tadpoles, *A 1:* 2, 4–5, 57

See also specific species

Taeniopygia guttata. See Zebra finches

Tailed frogs, A 1: 17–24

Tailless caecilians, A 3: 527–535

Tailless whip scorpions, *I 1:* 24–26, 24 (ill.), 25 (ill.)

Tailorbirds, *B 4:* 1051

Tails

break-off, *M 5:* 1173, 1183

lizards, *R 2:* 223, 244

prehensile, *M 3:* 527

See also specific species

Taipans, *R 2:* 416

Takahes, *B 2:* 356

Talamancan web-footed salamanders, *A 3:* 484–485, 484 (ill.), 485 (ill.)

Talas tuco-tucos, *M 5:* 1167

Taliabu masked owls, *B 3:* 559

Tall-grass wetland tapaculos, *B 4:* 847

Talpidae. *See* Desmans; Moles; Shrew moles

Tamanduas, *M 1:* 178–179, 180, 181, 195–197

Tamarins, M 3: 423, 424, 425, 426, 496–508

Tamias striatus. See Eastern chipmunks

The Taming of the Shrew (Shakespeare), *M 2:* 248

Tanagers, *B 4:* 789

Tanaidacea. *See* Tanaidaceans

Tanaidaceans, CM 155–159

Tangs

regal, *F* 230

yellow, *F* 327, 330–331, 330 (ill.), 331 (ill.)

Tanner's litter frogs, *A 2:* 311, 312, 313

Tantulocarida. *See* Tantulocaridans

Tantulocaridans, CM 204–208

Tapaculos, B 4: 845–849

Tapeworms, CJ 103–111

Tapiridae. *See* Tapirs

Tapirs, M 4: 848, 849–853, 865–873

Tapirus indicus. See Malayan tapirs

Tapirus terrestris. See Lowland tapirs

Tarantula hawks, *I 2:* 407–408, 407 (ill.), 408 (ill.)

Tarantulas and frogs, *A 3:* 373

Tardigrada. *See* Water bears

Tarpons, F 50–54

Tarsiers, M 3: 423, 424, 480–486

Tarsiidae. *See* Tarsiers

Tarsipedidae. *See* Honey possums

Tarsipes rostratus. See Honey possums

Tarsius bancanus. See Western tarsiers

Tarsius syrichta. See Philippine tarsiers

Tartaruga. *See* South American river turtles

Tasmacetus shepherdi. See Shepherd's beaked whales

Tasman beaked whales. *See* Shepherd's beaked whales

Tasmanian anaspid crustaceans, *CM* 106

Tasmanian barred bandicoots. *See* Eastern barred bandicoots

Tasmanian devils, M 1: 51, 53, 54, **56–63**, 61 (ill.), 62 (ill.)

Tasmanian emus, *B 1:* 27

Tasmanian tigers. *See* Tasmanian wolves

Tasmanian torrent midges, *I 2:* 341

Tasmanian wolves, M 1: 51, 54, **69–73**, 70 (ill.), 71 (ill.)

Tate's trioks, *M 1:* 163

Taudactylus eungellensis. See Eungella torrent frogs

Tawny frogmouths, *B 3:* 588–590, 588 (ill.), 589 (ill.)

Taxonomists, *B 4:* 861

Taxonomy, *F* 257, *M 1:* 173

Tayassu tajacu. See Collared peccaries

Tayassuidae. *See* Peccaries

Taylor, Edward H., *R 2:* 289

Tayras, *M 3:* 579, 614

Tchagra shrikes, *B 4:* 963

Teeth, carnassial, *M 3:* 581

Tegus, R 2: 235–242

Teiidae, R 2: 235–242

Telefomin possums, *M 1:* 118

Telson tails. *See* Proturans

Tenodera aridifolia sinensis. See Chinese mantids

Tenrec ecaudatus. See Common tenrecs

Tenrecidae. *See* Tenrecs

Tenrecs, M 2: 213, 214, 215, 216, **232–239**

Tent caterpillars, *I 2:* 372

Terek sandpipers, *B 2:* 454

Termes fatalis. See Linnaeus's snapping termites

Termites, I 1: 99, **117–134**, 136, *I 2:* 395

Terns, B 2: 395–398, 475–485

Terpsiphone viridis. See African paradise-flycatchers

Tineselfishes, *F* 230

Tinkerbirds, yellow-fronted, *B 3:* 752–753, 752 (ill.), 753 (ill.)

Tinkling frogs, *A 1:* 141

Tipula paludosa. See European marsh crane flies

Titis, *M 3:* 516–525

Titmice, *B 5:* 1164–1172

    long-tailed, *B 5:* 1151–1157

    penduline, *B 5:* 1158–1163

Tits. *See* Titmice

Toad-headed lizards, *R 1:* 147

Toad-like treefrogs, *A 3:* 333, 334

Toadfishes, *F* 181–186

Toadlets

    Australian, *A 1:* 139–151

    Madagascaran, *A 3:* 390–397

    three-toed, *A 2:* 190–197

Toads, *A 1:* 1–7

    fire-bellied, *A 1:* 25–43, 30 (ill.), 31 (ill.)

    Mesoamerican burrowing, *A 1:* 56–61, 59 (ill.), 60 (ill.)

    midwife, *A 1:* 44–55, 50 (ill.), 51 (ill.)

    spadefoot, *A 1:* 94–101

    Surinam, *A 1:* 62–76, 73–75, 73 (ill.), 74 (ill.)

    true, *A 2:* 198–217

Tobies, spotted, *F* 372–373, 372 (ill.), 373 (ill.)

Toco toucans, *B 3:* 763–764, 763 (ill.), 764 (ill.)

Todidae. *See* Todies

Todies, *B 3:* 653–657, 669–675, *B 4:* 988

Todus multicolor. See Cuban todies

Tok-tokkies, *I 2:* 295

Tokay geckos, *R 1:* 179

Tolypeutes. See Three-banded armadillos

Tomato frogs, *A 3:* 371

Tomicodon humeralis. See Sonora clingfishes

Tongan whistlers, *B 5:* 1132

Tongue worms, CM 237–241, 240 (ill.)

Tonkin snub-nosed monkeys, *M 3:* 537

Tooth-billed bowerbirds, *B 5:* 1380

Toothed whales, *M 4:* 705

Toothless sea cows, *M 4:* 829

Toros, *M 5:* 1182

Torrent-larks, *B 5:* 1360

Torrent salamanders, *A 3:* 471–475

Tortoise beetles, *I 2:* 296

Tortoises, *R 1:* 8–12, 87–94

Tortuga aplanada. See Central American river turtles

Tortuga blanca. See Central American river turtles

Tortuga plana. See Central American river turtles

Toucan barbets, *B 3:* 754–756, 754 (ill.), 755 (ill.)

Toucanets, *B 3:* 759

Toucans, *B 3:* 654, 725–729, 757–765

Toxotes jaculatrix. See Banded archerfishes

Trachelophorus giraffa. See Giraffe-necked weevils

Trachinoidei, *F* 292–298

Trachyboa species, *R 2:* 370, 371

Tragopan satyra. See Satyr tragopans

Tragulidae. *See* Chevrotains

Tragulus javanicus. See Lesser Malay mouse deer

Transparent reed frogs, *A 3:* 332

Trawlers, *B 1:* 44

Trawling, seaturtles and, *R 1:* 25

Tree boas, *R 2:* 343, 348–349, 348 (ill.), 349 (ill.)

Tree crickets, *I 1:* 168

Tree hyraxes, *M 4:* 821–822, 823–824, 823 (ill.), 824 (ill.)

Tree kangaroos, *M 1:* 26, 146–147, 146 (ill.), 147 (ill.)

Tree nighthawks. *See* Potoos

Tree pythons, green. *See* Green pythons

Tree shrew tenrecs, *M 2:* 234

Tree shrews, *M 2:* 263–268, *M 5:* 1202, 1224

Tree sloths

    three-toed, *M 1:* 178, 181, **189–194**

    two-toed, *M 1:* 178, 180, **183–188**

Tree snakes, brown, *R 2:* 402

Tree squirrels, *M 5:* 1008, 1009, 1010

Tree swallows, *B 4:* 914

Tree swifts, *B 3:* 610–611, 612–613, **624–629**

Treecreepers, *B 5:* 1182–1187, 1189

    See also Australian creepers

Treefrogs

    African, *A 3:* 331–349

    Amero-Australian, *A 2:* 259–286

    Asian, *A 3:* 350–367

Trematoda. *See* Flukes

Trematomus bernacchii. See Emerald notothens

Trepang, *CJ* 227

Triaenodes bicolor, I 2: 363–364, 363 (ill.), 364 (ill.)

Trichechidae. *See* Manatees

Trichechus manatus. See West Indian manatees

Trichobatrachus robustus. See Hairy frogs

Trichoglossus haematodus. See Rainbow lorikeets

Trichogramma species, *I 2:* 372

Trichoplax adhaerens, CJ 11

Trichoptera. *See* Caddisflies

Central American river, *R 1:* 39–43, 41 (ill.), 42 (ill.)

Eurasian pond and river, *R 1:* 58–63, 77

leatherback, *R 1:* 10, 24, 44–49, 47 (ill.), 48 (ill.)

neotropical wood, *R 1:* 58–63, 77

New World pond, *R 1:* 50–57, 77

pig-nose, *R 1:* 13–17, 16 (ill.), 17 (ill.)

seaturtles, *R 1:* 24–32

snapping, *R 1:* 10, **33–38**, 35 (ill.), 36 (ill.), 77

softshell, *R 1:* 8, 10, 95–100

Tusk shells, *CM* 289–292, 291 (ill.), 292 (ill.)

Tusked frogs, *A 1:* 129–131, 129 (ill.), 130 (ill.)

Tuxedo pincushion urchins, *CJ* 223–224, 223 (ill.), 224 (ill.)

Twig snakes, *R 2:* 402

Twisted-wing parasites, *I 2:* **315–319**, 318 (ill.), 319 (ill.)

Two-headed snakes. *See* Early blind snakes

Two-legged wormlizards, *R 1:* 200–202, 200 (ill.), 201 (ill.)

Two-lined salamanders, *A 3:* 486–488, 486 (ill.), 487 (ill.)

Two-toed anteaters. *See* Silky anteaters

Two-toed tree sloths, *M 1:* 178, 180, **183–188**

Tylototriton verrucosus. See Mandarin salamanders

Typhlonectes compressicauda. See Cayenne caecilians

Typhlophis species, *R 2:* 240

Typhlopidae. *See* Blind snakes

Typhlops depressicepts, R 2: 302

Typical antbirds, *B 4:* 836

Typical flycatchers, *B 4:* 1060

Typical nuthatches, *B 5:* 1173

Typical owls (Strigidae), *B 3:* 557, **564–573**

Typical swifts. *See* Swifts

Tyrannidae. *See* Tyrant flycatchers

Tyrannosaurus rex, R 1: 1, 2, 4

Tyraulets, *B 4:* 853

Tyrant flycatchers, *B 4:* **850–859**, 861, 872, 882

Tyrant-manakins, Wied's, *B 4:* 866

Tyrrhenian painted frogs, *A 1:* 45

Tyto alba. See Common barn owls

Tytonidae. *See* Barn owls

U

Uakaris, *M 3:* **516–525**

Uca pugilator. See Sand fiddler crabs

Ugandan squeakers, *A 2:* 310, 312, 313

Umbrella shadows, *B 1:* 150

Umbrellabirds, Amazonian, *B 4:* 877–878, 877 (ill.), 878 (ill.)

Unau. See Two-toed tree sloths

Uncia uncia. See Snow leopards

Underground species, *R 2:* 310 *See also* specific species

Ungaliophiidae, *R 2:* 369

Ungaliophis panamensis. See Southern bromeliad woodsnakes

Ungulates
    even-toed, *M 4:* 848, 887–891
    odd-toed, *M 4:* 848–853

United States Department of Agriculture (USDA)
    on red-winged blackbirds, *B 5:* 1274
    on rheas, *B 1:* 12

United States Fish and Wildlife Service. *See* Fish and Wildlife Service (U.S.)

Upupa epops. See Hoopoes

Upupidae. *See* Hoopoes

Uraeotyphlus oxyurus. See Red caecilians

Uraeotyphylidae. *See* Kerala caecilians

Urechis caupo. See Fat innkeeper worms

Uria aalge. See Common murres

Uropeltidae. *See* Shieldtail snakes

Uropeltis ocellatus, R 2: 315

Uropsylla tasmanica, I 2: 328

Ursidae. *See* Bears

Ursus americanus. See American black bears

Ursus maritimus. See Polar bears

U.S. Fish and Wildlife Service. *See* Fish and Wildlife Service (U.S.)

USDA. *See* United States Department of Agriculture

V

Valley pocket gophers, *M 5:* 1033–1035, 1033 (ill.), 1034 (ill.)

Vampire bats, *M 2:* 277, 279, 280, 346, 350–352, 350 (ill.), 351 (ill.)
    false, *M 2:* **323–329**
    spectral, *M 2:* 345, 347

Vampire squids, *CM* 303–304, 303 (ill.), 304 (ill.)

Vampyroteuthis infernalis. See Vampire squids

Wahnes's parotia, *B 5:* 1390

Wailing birds. *See* Limpkins

Walking catfish. *See* Hellbenders

Walkingsticks, common American, *I 1:* 202–204, 202 (ill.), 203 (ill.)

Wall creepers, *B 5:* **1173–1181**

Wall lizards, *R 2:* **221–227**

Wallabies, *M 1:* 99–104, **135–148**

Wallace's flying frogs, *A 3:* 350, 352

Walpurt. *See* Numbats

Walruses, *M 3:* 580, **684–689,** 686 (ill.), 687 (ill.)

Wandering gliders, *I 1:* 86–87, 86 (ill.), 87 (ill.)

Wandering violin mantids, *I 1:* 139–141, 139 (ill.), 140 (ill.)

Warblers, *B 4:* 789

    Australian, *B 4:* 1079–1086

    New World, *B 5:* 1258–1267

    Old World, *B 4:* 1050–1059

Warning colors. *See* Aposematic coloration

Wart snakes. *See* File snakes

Warthogs, *M 4:* 893

Warty hogs, Philippine, *M 4:* 894

Warty pigs, *M 4:* 894

Warty tree toads, *A 2:* 156

Washington giant earthworms, *CM* 19

Wasp-mimicking katydids, *I 1:* 169

Wasps, *I 2:* 339, **390–414**

Water bears, CM 61–65

Water beetles, *I 2:* 298, 301–302, 301 (ill.), 302 (ill.)

Water boas. *See* Green anacondas

Water boatmen, *I 2:* 240

Water buffaloes, *M 4:* 971–972, 971 (ill.), 972 (ill.)

Water bugs, giant, *I 2:* 239, 240, 248–249, 248 (ill.), 249 (ill.)

Water chevrotains, *M 4:* 928, 929

Water cobras, false, *R 2:* 401

Water dogs. *See* Hellbenders

Water dragons, *R 1:* 145, 146

Water filters, Bathynellaceans, *CM* 101

Water fleas, CM 75–86

Water frogs, *A 1:* **139–151**

Water-holding frogs, *A 1:* 2, *A 2:* 261, 278–280, 278 (ill.), 279 (ill.)

Water lily reed frogs. *See* Transparent reed frogs

Water loss, centipedes and, *I 2:* 417

Water moccasins. *See* Cottonmouths

Water monitors, Merten's, *R 2:* 280

Water opossums, *M 1:* 25–26, 33–35, 33 (ill.), 34 (ill.)

Water ouzels. *See* American dippers

Water quality

    pirate perches and, *F* 163

    stoneflies for, *I 1:* 94

Water rats, Australian, *M 5:* 998

Water scavengers, *I 2:* 294

Water scorpions, *I 2:* 238

Water shrews, *M 2:* 246, 247–248

    American, *M 2:* 252–253, 252 (ill.), 253 (ill.)

    Asiatic, *M 2:* 213–214

    elegant, *M 2:* 248

    European, *M 2:* 247

Water skinks, *R 2:* 250

Water snakes, *R 1:* 140, *R 2:* 400, 402

Water striders, *I 2:* 238

Water turkeys. *See* American anhingas

Waterthrushes. *See* American dippers

Wattle-eyes, *B 4:* 1062, 1067

Wattlebirds, New Zealand, *B 5:* **1353–1359**

Wattled cranes, *B 2:* 319

Wattled curassows, *B 2:* 286–287, 286 (ill.), 287 (ill.)

Waxbills, *B 5:* **1296–1305**

Waxwings, *B 4:* **979–987,** 988

Weasel lemurs. *See* Sportive lemurs

Weasels, *M 3:* 578, 579, **614–627,** 637, *M 5:* 1206

Weaverfinches. *See* Grassfinches; Waxbills

Weavers, *B 5:* **1306–1317**

Web-foot frogs, *A 3:* 391, 392, 393

Web-footed dwarf litter frogs, *A 1:* 80

Webless toothed toads. *See* Schmidt's lazy toads

Webs, spider, *I 1:* 17

Webspinners, *I 2:* **211–215**

Webworms, *I 2:* 372

Wedgebills, *B 4:* 1099, 1100, 1101

Weeper capuchins, *M 3:* 493–495, 493 (ill.), 494 (ill.)

Weeverfishes, F 292–298

Weevils, *I 2:* **289–314**

West African screeching frogs, *A 2:* 311, 313–314

West Atlantic stalked crinoids, *CJ* 185–186, 185 (ill.), 186 (ill.)

West Indian manatees, *M 4:* 844–846, 844 (ill.), 845 (ill.)

West Indian sloths, *M 1:* **183–188**

Western banded geckos, *R 1:* 181–182, 181 (ill.), 182 (ill.)

Western barbastelles, *M 2:* 415–416, 415 (ill.), 416 (ill.)

White helmet-shrikes, *B 4:* 965–967, 965 (ill.), 966 (ill.)

White-lipped peccaries, *M 4:* 903

White-mantled barbets, *B 3:* 749

White-naped cranes, *B 2:* 319

White-naped tits, *B 5:* 1166

White-necked puffbirds, *B 3:* 741–743, 741 (ill.), 742 (ill.)

White rhinoceroses, *M 4:* 848, 850, 874, 876, 883–885, 883 (ill.), 884 (ill.)

White-rumped sandpipers, *B 2:* 455

White sharks, *F* 15–16, 15 (ill.), 16 (ill.)

White-spotted puffers, *F* 370–371, 370 (ill.), 371 (ill.)

White-spotted reed frogs, *A 3:* 332

White storks, *B 1:* 146

White sturgeons, *F* 34

White-tailed deer, *M 4:* 889–890, 943–945, 943 (ill.), 944 (ill.)

White-tailed plovers, *B 2:* 445

White-tailed swallows, *B 4:* 915

White-tailed tropicbirds, *B 1:* 105–107, 105 (ill.), 106 (ill.)

White-throated capuchins, *M 3:* 491–492, 491 (ill.), 492 (ill.)

White-throated dippers. *See* Eurasian dippers

White-throated fantails, *B 4:* 1106, 1107–1108, 1110–1111, 1110 (ill.), 1111 (ill.)

White-throated gerygones, *B 4:* 1080

White-throated tits, *B 5:* 1152, 1153

White-throated toucans, *B 3:* 759

White-throated treecreepers, *B 5:* 1145, 1147

White-toothed shrews, *M 2:* 248

White whales. *See* Belugas

White-whiskered spider monkeys, *M 3:* 527

White-winged choughs, *B 5:* 1360

White-winged cotingas, *B 4:* 874

White-winged cuckoo-shrikes, *B 4:* 936, 937

White-winged nightjars, *B 3:* 577, 604

White-winged sandpipers, *B 2:* 456

White-winged wood ducks, *B 2:* 259

Whitefishes, *F* 127

Whiteflies, *I 2:* 236, 237, 241–242, 241 (ill.), 242 (ill.)

Whooping cranes, *B 2:* 318, 319, 334, 335

Wide-headed rottenwood termites, *I 1:* 132–133, 132 (ill.), 133 (ill.)

Widowbirds, *B 5:* 1306–1307

Wied's tyrant-manakins, *B 4:* 866

Wild cats, *M 3:* 581, 658

Wild dogs, African, *M 3:* 583

Wild meat, *M 4:* 889

Wild Meat, Livelihoods Security and Conservation in the Tropics project, *M 4:* 889

Wild pigs, Eurasian, *M 4:* 899–900, 899 (ill.), 900 (ill.)

Wild turkeys, *B 2:* 266, 295, 296–297, 296 (ill.), 297 (ill.)

Wildebeest, black, *M 4:* 976–977, 976 (ill.), 977 (ill.)

Wildlife Foundation (Africa), *M 4:* 876

Wildlife Preservation Trust (Jersey), *R 2:* 365

Wildlife Protection Act (Jamaica), *M 5:* 1189

Wildlife Service (New Zealand), *B 5:* 1355

Wilhelm rainforest frogs, **A** *3:* 376–377, 376 (ill.), 377 (ill.)

Willie wagtails, *B 4:* 1106–1107, 1108, 1109, 1112–1114, 1112 (ill.), 1113 (ill.)

Willow ptarmigans, *B 2:* 298–299, 298 (ill.), 299 (ill.)

Wilson's birds of paradise, *B 5:* 1390

Wilson's storm-petrels, *B 1:* 64–66, 64 (ill.), 65 (ill.)

Wingless wood cockroaches, *I 1:* 117

Winter wrens, *B 4:* 1045–1046, 1045 (ill.), 1046 (ill.)

Wire-tailed manakins, *B 4:* 869–870, 869 (ill.), 870 (ill.)

Wirsing, Aaron, *M 4:* 834

Wolf-eels, *F* 256, 281, 282, 283–284, 283 (ill.), 284 (ill.)

Wolf herrings, *F* 73

Wolverines, *M 3:* 637

Wolves, *M 3:* 581, **583–592**
  See also Tasmanian wolves

Wombats, *M 1:* 99–104, 106, **111–115**

Wonga pigeons, *B 3:* 509

Wood-boring beetles, *I 2:* 293, 298

Wood ducks, *B 2:* 258–259, 258 (ill.), 259 (ill.)

Wood frogs, *A 1:* 4, **A** *2:* 287, 289–290

Wood-partridge, bearded, *B 2:* 305

Wood pigeons, *B 3:* 505, 509

Wood snipes, *B 2:* 456

Wood storks, *B 1:* 166, 168–170, 168 (ill.), 169 (ill.)

Wood ticks, Rocky Mountain, *I 1:* 21–23, 21 (ill.), 22 (ill.)

Wood turtles, neotropical, *R 1:* 51, **58–63,** 77

Woodcocks, *B 2:* 454, 455, 456

Woodcreepers, *B 4:* 830–835

Woodhoopoes, *B 3:* 653, 654, 707–713

Woodlark cuscuses, *M 1:* 116

Woodlarks, *B 4:* 902

Woodlice, CM 174–184, 233

Woodpeckers, *B 3:* 725–729, 766, 768, **774–788**

Woodsnakes, *R 2:* 369–374

Woodswallows, *B 5:* 1366–1371

Woodworms. *See* Thrips

Woolly horseshoe bats, *M 2:* 331

Woolly lemurs, *M 3:* 459

Woolly monkeys, *M 3:* 526, 527, 533–534, 533 (ill.), 534 (ill.)

Woolly opossums, *M 1:* 28

Worcester's buttonquails, *B 2:* 328

World Conservation Union (IUCN) Red List of Threatened Species, *A 3:* 400, *M 5:* 1183

    on aardvarks, *M 4:* 807

    on African side-necked turtles, *R 1:* 72

    on African treefrogs, *A 3:* 337–338

    on Afro-American river turtles, *R 1:* 83

    on Agamidae, *R 1:* 147

    on agoutis, *M 5:* 1155

    on Albert's lyrebirds, *B 4:* 893

    on alligators, *R 1:* 116

    on American crocodiles, *R 1:* 128

    on American mud and musk turtles, *R 1:* 66

    on Amero-Australian treefrogs, *A 2:* 264, 267

    on amphipods, *CM* 187

    on amphiumas, *A 3:* 497

    on anaspidaceans, *CM* 106

    on anemones and corals, *CJ* 29

    on anglerfishes, *F* 188

    on Anguidae, *R 2:* 262–263

    on anoplans and enoplans, *CJ* 113

    on anteaters, *M 1:* 197

    on arachnids, *I 1:* 18

    on armadillos, *M 1:* 205

    on armored chameleons, *R 1:* 163

    on Asian tailed caecilians, *A 3:* 513

    on Asian toadfrogs, *A 1:* 80–81, 83, 85, 88, 92

    on Asian treefrogs, *A 3:* 355, 356–357, 363

    on Asiatic giant salamanders and hellbenders, *A 3:* 422, 425–426,

    on Asiatic salamanders, *A 3:* 412, 418

    on asities, *B 4:* 803

    on Atlantic cods, *F* 178

    on Australian ground frogs, *A 1:* 127–128, 131

    on Australian toadlets and water frogs, *A 1:* 141, 142–143, 150, *A 2:* 180

    on Australo-American side-necked turtles, *R 1:* 20

    on bald uakaris, *M 3:* 522

    on barbourulas, *A 1:* 28–29

    on bats, *M 2:* 280

    on beavers, *M 5:* 1025

    on beetles, *I 2:* 298, 311

    on big-headed turtles, *R 1:* 80

    on birch mice, *M 5:* 1047

    on bivalves, *CM* 276

    on black guans, *B 2:* 285

    on blennies, *F* 300

    on blind snakes, *R 2:* 305

    on boas, *R 2:* 344

    on bony tongues, *F* 47–48

    on Bornean orangutans, *M 3:* 567

    on Bovidae, *M 4:* 970

    on broadbills, *B 4:* 795

    on buttonquails, *B 2:* 328

    on caddisflies, *I 2:* 361–362

    on caecilians, *A 3:* 504

    on caimans, *R 1:* 116

    on camels, *M 4:* 918

    on Canidae, *M 3:* 584

    on capuchins, *M 3:* 488

    on carnivores, *M 3:* 581–582

    on carps, *F* 85

    on cassowaries, *B 1:* 20

    on catfishes, *F* 102

    on cats, *M 3:* 658

    on centipedes, *I 2:* 418

    on Central American river turtles, *R 1:* 42

    on chameleons, *R 1:* 159, 163, 165

    on characins, *F* 93

    on Charadriiformes, *B 2:* 397–398

    on chevrotains, *M 4:* 929

    on *Chiloporter eatoni, I 1:* 77

    on chimpanzees, *M 3:* 573

    on chinchilla rats, *M 5:* 1178

    on chinchillas, *M 5:* 1131, 1134

    on cicadas, *I 2:* 247

    on civets, *M 3:* 629–630

    on clam worms, *CM* 3–4

    on clawed frogs, *A 1:* 65–66

    on coelacanths, *F* 22, 24

    on colobus, *M 3:* 539

    on colubrids, *R 2:* 402

    on common bentwing bats, *2:* 420

    on common chameleons, *R 1:* 165

    on copepods, *CM* 222–223

    on cranes, *B 2:* 335

    on crocodiles, *R 1:* 126, 128, 130–131

World Conservation Union
(IUCN) Red List of
Threatened Species,
(*continued*)
on pocket mice, *M 5:* 1038
on poison frogs, **A** *2:*
224–225, 228, 231, 234
on prairie dogs, *M 5:* 1016
on proboscis monkeys, *M
3:* 542
on Procyonidae, *M 3:* 606
on pufferfishes, *F* 367
on pumas, *M 3:* 667
on pygopods, *R 1:* 180
on pythons, *R 2:* 355
on rabbits, *M 5:*
1214–1215
on rails, *B 2:* 358–359
on rainbowfishes, *F* 199
on ratites, *B 1:* 7
on rays, *F* 10
on red-crowned cranes, *B
2:* 342
on red pandas, *M 3:*
610–612
on rheas, *B 1:* 13
on rhesus macaques, *M 3:*
427
on rhinoceroses, *M 4:* 882,
885
on rock-crawlers, *I 1:* 154
on rodents, *M 5:*
1000–1001
on sakis, *M 3:* 517
on salamanders and newts,
A *3:* 402
on salmons, *F* 128
on sand worms, *CM* 3–4
on Scombroidei, *F* 335
on Scorpaeniformes, *F*
248–249
on sea lions, *M 3:* 674, 682
on sea urchins and sand
dollars, 214
on seaturtles, *R 1:* 26, 31
on sengis, *M 5:* 1225,
1227

on serows, *M 4:* 984
on Seychelles frogs, **A** *1:*
117, 120, 123
on sharks, *F* 10, 16
on shearwaters, *B 1:* 55
on short-tailed bats, *M 2:*
373, 376
on shovel-nosed frogs, **A**
2: 326
on shrew opossums, *M 1:*
40
on shrews, *M 2:* 249
on shrikes, *B 4:* 964
on siamangs, *M 3:* 560
on Siberian musk deer, *M
4:* 936
on silversides, *F* 199
on Sirenia, *M 4:* 831
on skates, *F* 10
on skinks, *R 2:* 251–252
on slit-faced bats, *M 2:*
318
on snakes, *R 1:* 143
on snapping turtles, *R 1:*
34
on snow leopards, *M 3:*
669
on softshell turtles, *R 1:*
97
on solenodons, *M 2:* 242,
244
on South American river
turtles, *R 1:* 86
on southern cassowaries,
B 1: 22
on spadefoot toads, **A** *1:*
83, 85, 88, 92–93, 97
on spider monkeys, *M 3:*
527
on spiny rats, *M 5:* 1184
on splitjaw snakes, *R 2:*
366–367
on sportive lemurs, *M 3:*
468
on springhares, *M 5:* 1080
on squeakers and cricket
frogs, **A** *2:* 314–315

on squirrel monkeys, *M 3:*
488
on squirrels, *M 5:* 1010
on stoneflies, *I 1:* 94–95
on sturgeons, *F* 33–34
on sucker-footed bats, *M
2:* 39
on sunbirds, *B 5:* 1210
on Surinam toads, **A** *1:*
65–66
on swallows, *B 4:* 915
on swamp and spiny eels,
F 243
on swifts, *B 3:* 613, 617
on tailess caecilians, **A** *3:*
529
on tamarins, *M 3:*
497–498, 501
on tarsiers, *M 3:* 481, 483,
486
on Teiidae, *R 2:* 237
on tenrecs, *M 2:* 234
on theocostracans, *CM* 198
on three-toed toadlets, **A**
2: 192–193
on thumbless bats, *M 2:*
384
on tinamous, *B 1:* 7
on titis, *M 3:* 517, 524
on toadfishes, *F* 183
on torrent salamanders, **A**
3: 475
on tortoises, *R 1:* 11,
88–89
on toucans, *B 3:* 759,
761–762
on triggerfishes, *F* 367
on trogons, *B 3:* 646
on troutperches, *F* 163
on true frogs, **A** *2:*
291–292, 295, 298, 300
on true seals, *M 3:* 691
on true toads, **A** *2:*
202–204, 206–207, 210,
216
on tuataras, *R 1:* 135, 137
on tubeworms, *CM* 3–4

Yellow-bellied fantails, *B 4:* 1108

Yellow-bellied gliders, *M 1:* 163

Yellow-bellied sapsuckers, *B 3:* 784–785, 784 (ill.), 785 (ill.)

Yellow-bellied sunbird-asities, *B 4:* 801, 802, 803

Yellow-bellied toads, **A** *1:* 37–40, 37 (ill.), 38 (ill.)

Yellow-billed cotingas, *B 4:* 874

Yellow-breasted birds of paradise, *B 5:* 1390

Yellow-breasted capuchins, *M 3:* 488

Yellow-breasted chats, *B 5:* 1261–1262, 1261 (ill.), 1262 (ill.)

Yellow-breasted toucanets, *B 3:* 759

Yellow chats, *B 4:* 1088, 1089

Yellow-crowned bishops, *B 5:* 1309

Yellow-crowned bulbuls, *B 4:* 945

Yellow-crowned gonoleks, *B 4:* 962

Yellow-eyed penguins, *B 1:* 73

Yellow fever mosquitoes, *I 2:* 342–343, 342 (ill.), 343 (ill.)

Yellow-footed rock wallabies, *M 1:* 101

Yellow-fronted tinkerbirds, *B 3:* 752–753, 752 (ill.), 753 (ill.)

Yellow golden moles, *M 2:* 226

Yellow-headed vultures, *B 1:* 175–176

Yellow jackets, *I 2:* 393, 395

Yellow-legged kassinas, **A** *3:* 332

Yellow-legged tinamous, *B 1:* 7

Yellow-legged treefrogs. *See* Yellow-legged kassinas

Yellow-margined box turtles, *R 1:* 61–63, 61 (ill.), 62 (ill.)

Yellow monitors, *R 2:* 282

Yellow mud turtles, *R 1:* 65

Yellow-rumped honeyguides, *B 3:* 768

Yellow-rumped thornbills, *B 4:* 1082–1083, 1082 (ill.), 1083 (ill.)

Yellow-spotted nicators, *B 4:* 945

Yellow-spotted night lizards, *R 2:* 215, 216, 217

Yellow-streaked bulbuls, *B 4:* 944

Yellow-streaked tenrecs, *M 2:* 237–238, 237 (ill.), 238 (ill.)

Yellow-striped reed frogs, **A** *3:* 332

Yellow-tailed woolly monkeys, *M 3:* 527

Yellow tangs, *F* 327, 330–331, 330 (ill.), 331 (ill.)

Yellow-throated leafbirds, *B 4:* 956

Yellow tits, *B 5:* 1166

Yellow wagtails, *B 4:* 929

Yellow-winged bats, *M 2:* 324, 325

Yellowheads, *B 4:* 1084–1085, 1084 (ill.), 1085 (ill.), *B 5:* 1132

Yellowstone National Park, *M 3:* 587

Yemen accentors, *B 4:* 993

Yerbua capensis. See Springhares

Yucatecan shovel-headed treefrogs, **A** *2:* 276–277, 276 (ill.), 277 (ill.)

Yungas redbelly toads, **A** *2:* 199, 200, 201

Yunnan moustache toads. *See* Ailao moustache toads

Z

Zalophus californianus. See California sea lions

Zalophus wollebaeki. See Galápagos sea lions

Zambezi blind snakes, *R 2:* 302

Zanclus cornutus. See Moorish idols

Zapata wrens, *B 4:* 1039

Zebra finches, *B 5:* 1298, 1301–1302, 1301 (ill.), 1302 (ill.)

Zebra jumping spiders, *I 1:* 29–31, 29 (ill.), 30 (ill.)

Zebra mussels, *CM* 276, 279–281, 279 (ill.), 280 (ill.)

Zebra-tailed lizards, *R 1:* 168

Zebrafishes, *F* 85

Zebras, *M 4:* 848–850, 852, **854–864**

Zebrasoma flavescens. See Yellow tangs

Zeiformes. *See* Dories

Zenaida macroura. See American mourning doves

Zenkerella species, *M 5:* 1069

Zeus (God), *CM* 307

Zimmermann's poison frogs, *A 2:* 219

Ziphiidae. *See* Beaked whales

Zitting cisticolas, *B 4:* 1053–1054, 1053 (ill.), 1054 (ill.)

Zoarces americanus. See Ocean pouts

Zoarcoidei, *F* 281–287

Zonocerus variegatus. See Variegated grasshoppers

Zootermopsis laticeps. See Wide-headed rottenwood termites

Zorapterans, *I 2:* **216–221**

Zorotypus hubbardi. See Hubbard's angel insects

Zosteropidae. *See* White-eyes

Zosterops japonicus. See Japanese white-eyes

Zuberbühler, Klaus, *B 3:* 539